How the

Gets in

How the Light Gets In

short stories

Brian E. Pearson

Anglican Book Centre
Toronto, Canada

1999
Anglican Book Centre
600 Jarvis Street
Toronto, Ontario
M4Y 2J6

Cover illustration by Lester Clarke.
Author photo by Marilyn McEwan of Aperture Overtures, Ucluelet, British Columbia.

Canadian Cataloguing in Publication Data

Pearson, Brian E.
　How the light gets in: short stories

ISBN 1-55126-258-4

1. Christian fiction, Canadian (English). * I. Title.

PS8581.E382H68 1999　　　C813'.54　　　C99-932343-1
PR9199.3.P38H68 1999

To the memory of
ARTHUR MYERS PEARSON
(1924–1999)
and
DORENE RUTH PEARSON
(1925–1991)

through whom the light shone

*The title of this book
echoes a line from the
song "Anthem" by Leonard Cohen.*

Contents

Acknowledgements

This book is in your hands because along the way there were people who encouraged me to write it, though some could not have foreseen it would lead to this. Among them:

Arthur and Dorene Pearson, my parents, to whom this book is dedicated — I hope they would be pleased;

the five parishes (or seven congregations) I have served, who have always made allowances for a preaching style that is often, ah, conversational, thereby preparing the way for the telling of stories;

Brian Murray for wondering, and then for persisting in wondering, why my creative energies could not be channelled through my work (and whose own storytelling skills ensured that the "Leg Sandwich" sermon illustration at my ordination would long outlive the memories of the ordination itself);

Alexandra Caverly Lowery, who, through one particularly lost period, watched my body language as I described, on the one hand, "the church" (right hand extended, palm forward, as if to stop a freight train) and, on the other, "all these things I want to do" (left hand extended, fingers rubbing together, as if to ignite so many brush fires), thus helping me to get started;

Joyce Carlson, who helped me find and then defend my narrative voice, and who contributed the real-life anecdote that became the story "Chicken Soup," in this collection;

Audrey Conard, who received my early drafts as if they were my children, welcoming them, warming them up with hot soup, replacing a missing button or two, helping them to find their snowsuits and overshoes, and then returning them home to me, better;

Robert Maclennan, Publishing Manager of the Anglican Book Centre, who graciously accepted the drafts I slipped to him at a national committee meeting, liked them and set in motion the turning of wheels that has led to the publication of this book (thus proving what a friend once observed, that national church committees *really are* just job fairs for clergy;

Vianney (Sam) Carriere, Church House's editor of Print Resources, whose enthusiasm for the project bolstered my own, and whose "ear" for good writing led to many incisive observations and helpful suggestions; the collection is much better as a result;

my children — Heather, Robert, and Benjamin — whose own creative energy daily both inspires and exhausts me, and who shoved over to let Dad hog the computer on his writing days, and on good many an evening as well;

finally, and above all, *Sandra,* my friend and life-partner, who long ago said, simply, "You should write."

I have. Thanks to you all.

Introduction

It was a pastoral visit gone awry, one thing leading to another. The woman's husband came home unexpectedly. The young curate leapt up, punched the startled man in the nose and fled out the door.

Storytelling can be like that.

Jesus was a storyteller. He was not a theologian, though he spoke in a reasonable way about God. Nor was he a motivational speaker, though he did seem to have a way with words. As far as we can tell, he mostly told stories, stories that did his work for him, stories that lived on in the memories of his hearers long after he himself was gone, stories that gathered a life of their own.

We preachers are often on the verge of storytelling. We provide examples from history. We illustrate a point with reference to popular culture. We might even dare to make something up by way of a metaphor. But ordinarily we stop short of telling stories. We feel it is our duty first and foremost to teach theology, to promote correct understanding, and not to get carried away.

Which is what stories do, of course. They carry us away. They find us where we are, pick us up and, one thing leading to another, take us off somewhere else altogether. This is disturbing for those of us who bought the ticket, thinking we knew where we were getting off. Stories serve to remind us that, wherever it is we think we're going, we're not very likely to end up there. And that if we did, how sad.

The first of these stories was told in the context of a Sunday sermon. It was about the Lucas brothers, a story called "Forgiveness" in this collection.

It was a Saturday evening early in the fall. I was moody as usual, coming off my summer vacation and chafing at the bit and bridle of a new season. The gospel reading for the next day had to do with Peter asking Jesus, "How often should I forgive? As many as seven times?" So the theme for the sermon, of course, would have to be, "Not seven times, but, I tell you, seventy-seven times." Ya, ya, we're supposed to forgive one another. But I was having a hard time dishing that one up again.

Meanwhile, over the summer, while visiting my wife's relatives, dairy farmers in the Ottawa Valley, we had heard the sad story of two brothers who'd had some sort of falling out. They never spoke to one another again. It is not an uncommon story, all families being to some extent dysfunctional or, at the very least, difficult. But I had come home haunted by it, wishing I knew more.

So I wondered: what if, instead of the usual sermon, I just told this story, changing the names and filling in the blanks with fictional details? Only, I would not say it was a story. I would just start talking and end up in this prolonged narrative about two brothers. It would be off the cuff, anecdotal, a bit rough around the edges, as in any case it would have to be, given the lateness of the hour.

So that's what I did. I did not say, "Jesus said we ought to forgive one another and here's a story to illustrate the point." I just read the gospel for the day, went to my usual place at the chancel step, and began talking about these two guys I once knew, the Lucas brothers.

The attentiveness of the congregation, right off, was startling. Perhaps they knew people like this in their own lives. Perhaps their attention was caught by the lure of what sounded like some juicy gossip. But they hung off every word. As I approached the story's sad conclusion — Margaret, seeing her husband coming down the stairs in his suit jacket, saying to him simply, "Oh, Dan!" — people were dabbing at their eyes with tissues.

I had a hard time myself, when it was over. I wasn't sure what had just happened. Was it preaching or was it performance? Was it truth-telling or some sort of emotional manipulation? I didn't know, and that disturbed me.

One thing was certain, though: people wanted to talk about it. They wanted to know more about these brothers. And that got them telling stories of their own, stories about mothers-in-law and family quarrels and, though they may not have used the words, stories about grace and redemption. It was as if we had all been picked up from the bus stop, transfers in hand, and dropped off in a different place altogether. We were changed.

So I wrote more stories and began slipping them into the sermon slot from time to time. I'm still at it, in fact. But I pull back from doing it too often. The truth is, I am a coward. Even for the storyteller, these things have a way of gathering a momentum of their own and, like the pastoral visit gone awry, taking off in unexpected directions. It generates more power than I care to handle, at least on a regular basis. It seems I, too, want to know where I'm going to end up most Sundays.

Anyway, it's time to bundle some of these stories together, along with a few that for discretion's sake could not be told from a pulpit, and let them out to speak for themselves. Some are little more than vignettes, really. Some are probably more essay than story. Some are merely the recasting of stories already told by Jesus himself.

But if they are a way back to that master storyteller, who after all knew a thing or two about messing up people's destinations, who indeed was not only wordsmith but also divine Word, then these stories have a purpose, and I am pleased to tell them — one thing leading to another.

Country Kitchens

A snowy eiderdown settled on the house last night as we slept. You could tell the moment you awoke. There wasn't a sound, just the dull far-off drone of the furnace. The last few flakes were still falling as I stood with my coffee at the front window.

On mornings like this I make porridge for the family. Someday they will thank me for this. I lace it to make it more palatable for them — a little salt for zest, bran flakes for texture, maple syrup for taste. Of course, to them it is still oatmeal. But to me it is food for the soul. It is hot in your mouth and warm going down. It sticks to your ribs, as my grandmother used to say, which was somehow a comforting thought. But it doesn't have the same effect when I repeat this to my children.

What an extravagant world God has made! A world you cannot only touch and see and smell and hear, but also taste. It is no accident that Jesus, wanting to a leave a sign for his disciples, left them a meal: warm bread fried in the pan, and sweet wine.

He knew what he was doing. This was no cerebral love, as if his chief accomplishment on the cross would be an improved *concept*. It was an embodied love, as good for the belly as for the soul.

In divinity school they taught us all we needed to know about the eucharist, the centre-piece of Christian worship that has evolved over generations from the Last Supper. In a series of non-credit courses taught by the dean, we learned how to chant (a course we called DeanSing), how to enunciate properly (DeanSpeak), and how to preside at the Holy Mysteries (Priestcraft). We folded our hands together and tucked in our thumbs. We raised our arms — but not too high — to "hold" the prayers of the people. We held one hand to the heart while making the sign of the cross with the other — fingers straight, thumb out of sight, slicing the air, not waving to the people. But I didn't learn a thing about food until my first parish.

The parish of St. Jude's is in farming country, dairy farming to be exact. People there are not sentimental about food. How could they be, when they eat what they grow, including Bessie and Ferdinand? They eat to get the job done.

But though they're not sentimental about food, neither do they take it lightly. A pot luck supper is a minefield for a new minister: two eight-foot-long folding tables joined end to end and, adorned with a plastic gingham runner, crammed with offerings from every kitchen in the parish — casseroles and lasagna and jelly-mould salads and cake and pie and fruit bread. The natural temptation, of course, is to overdo it.

I once piled my plate high with a sample from every dish. When I had worked my way to the bottom and felt ready to explode, I still had one helping of lasagna left. Discreetly, I placed a paper napkin over it and gave it a heave under the sink. Two years later Flo Templeton got mad at me about a sermon or something, and then added the zinger. "Besides," she said, her pointed finger shaking with rage, "I saw what you did, how you chose my lasagna from all the others and threw it in the waste bin. You think I didn't see, but I did." Years later I am still trying to come up with a response.

I learned early on that an unannounced parish visit around four in the afternoon led to roast beef and mashed potatoes just as surely as the new day led to morning chores. It would have caused offense to rebuff their hospitality, especially when they insisted it was just one more potato in the pot. It was also true, of course, that the pastoral call, in the strictest sense, lost some of its focus around the big kitchen table. This was not a time for conversation. It was a time to pass the peas, pass the butter, pass the corn, pass the pie.

Had I missed the secret of the country kitchen I would have missed the heartbeat of my congregation. This is not a secret you learn by calling ahead and making an appointment, as they do in the city. A formal pastoral call in a rural parish never gets you to the kitchen. You might pass by the dining-room, the hub of the farming operation, the table piled high with bills and papers, with a calculator and now, likely, a computer. But they take you instead to the front room, a formal parlour they never use themselves. It is a room reserved for clergy, and for undertakers.

Lounging awkwardly in an antique straight back chair, trying to look casual, you make conversation. You ask how the farming's going. It's going fine, thank you, but one never knows what'll happen tomorrow. You ask about the photographs on the piano. You get names and family connections. Someone plays hockey, someone else has gone off to college.

As the ticking of the clock between the long silences announces that a mere twenty minutes have passed, you slap your knee and say you have to be on your way. Your hostess is stunned. So soon? She has made blackcurrant sweet tarts for you. Please, you must stay. She'll just go and reboil the kettle and make some tea. It won't take a minute.

It takes more than a minute. You realize you have violated some unspoken rule, like, a proper pastoral visit in these parts never takes less than an hour and the tea is served after forty-five minutes. These are hard things for a city-bred boy to learn.

But mealtime in the country is different. One of my first country meals was at the home of my neighbours, the Browns. They were in their seventies, living in town and enjoying the simple pleasures of retirement. Alf had spent much of his life farming, though he never owned a farm of his own. For the last ten years he had been custodian at the district high school. Theirs had not been an easy life, but Ina had managed to put away something every year, even while they were raising their children; so that now they owned their own home and were able to live comfortably, happily active in the church and in the busy affairs of the community.

It was my second or third week in the parish, and Ina had invited me over for dinner following church on Sunday. I would have to keep an eye on the clock, as I had arranged a visit with Daisy Youngman later that afternoon. But I accepted her invitation and looked forward to their hospitality.

I was not disappointed. While Ina made meal preparations in the kitchen, Alf brought out his accordion. I sat at the piano and together we muddled our way through a few old hymns and war songs. He began telling me stories from the war, but then Ina called us to the table. She had set out her finest bone china. Alf and I took our places and Ina re-emerged from the kitchen with a roast chicken, arranged on a platter with roasted potatoes and carrots. More serving dishes arrived: peas, mashed potatoes, gravy, celery, olives, buns and butter.

We shared stories, mine sounding so slight and insubstantial compared to theirs. Alf had been one of Dr. Bernardo's "home children," orphans taken from the streets and orphanages of pre-war England and sent out to adoptive households throughout the Commonwealth. Most of the children became little more than indentured servants, working for their room and board until they were old enough to break free and start a life of their own.

Alf had been taken in by the Whittakers, who had a dairy farm south of town. He had grown up alongside Earl Whittaker, who was his own age and who might have been like a brother to Alf had old Mr. Whittaker allowed it. Instead, Alf did chores while the family sat down to eat, taking his meals alone after they were done.

I had seconds and thirds of everything. I pushed my chair back from the table, but then Ina brought out a freshly baked peach pie, and served up huge slabs for Alf and me, with double dollops of vanilla ice-cream. I was slowing down, a sleepy haze descending on me, as Alf wondered aloud about kids nowadays and old world values and things he just couldn't understand.

Back in the living-room again, over cups of tea and biscuits with cheese, Ina offered me measured advice about St. Jude's. There were people — good well-meaning people, mind you — but people I ought to be wary of, some who would be nice to my face but then cause trouble behind my back, others who would try to run things their own way. But I was their new minister, and I should do what I thought was right. She and Alf would support me.

I took my leave about three o'clock, feeling bloated and drowsy, all but rolling down the road to Daisy Youngman's house. I had not met Daisy before. She was elderly and, I understood, infirm. She could no longer make it out to church, but several people had told me it would be important for me to call on her. So I arrived and rang the bell. After a few moments I could hear the *shuffle, thump, shuffle, thump,* of a walker making its way to the door.

Daisy was indeed old, her body badly hunched over. Yet her eyes shone as she greeted me. She had me sit in the parlour while she got a few things ready in the kitchen. She asked me to pour myself a glass of sherry from a decanter that had been placed on a TV table beside the chair. I asked if there was anything I could do to help, but she was clearly determined to serve me.

I sipped at the sherry, taking in the details of the room. Her daughter was reeve of the town, but there was no indication of that here. Instead there were pictures of grandchildren, a display of birthday cards, some framed needlepoints, and doilies everywhere. The room was warm. I could feel myself slowly sinking, deeper, deeper into the chair.

Daisy was speaking to me from the doorway. I awoke with a jolt. She was inviting me into the kitchen. Rising unsteadily, I could smell something cooking. Two places were set at the kitchen table. She insisted I be seated. And then, making her way over to the oven, she bent over, opened the oven door, and produced a triumphant platter — roast chicken, with carrots and potatoes.

I got up and helped bring the meal to the table, holding her chair as she sat down opposite my place. She looked exhausted. She said she didn't have much of an appetite herself. But she had raised three children and she knew how to feed them, so would I please say a blessing and then go ahead myself?

Sometimes people have asked my opinion: should they take communion twice the same day, as when someone is server at the early eucharist and then returns with their family later for the main service? Isn't that an abuse of the sacrament, to receive it more than once?

For me, the matter is fairly simple. Do you eat more than three meals a day? Not without regretting it. But if, after you have had your own dinner, you should drop in at your neighbour's and they ask you to join them out on the porch for a cup of coffee, you would not refuse the invitation. You take the coffee, and maybe a piece of cake, too, not because you need it, but because it is the right thing to do. It honours your friendship.

So also with God's grace. Will I refuse the costly gift of Christ's body and blood because it is more than I need, indeed more than I will ever need? Do I decline the offer, saying, "That's awfully kind of you, you really have gone to a lot of trouble, but I've had enough already. Perhaps some other time"?

No. I ate the chicken. I stuffed down the roast potatoes. I helped myself to the carrots and to the gravy. And then when Daisy toddled back to the counter and removed a tea towel from a freshly baked peach pie, I exclaimed that no one could turn down such a lovely pie as that. I "passed" on the ice-cream, though.

Daisy died several months later. While she lay in the hospital I went to see her. She was rolled up in a fetal position, her hands curling in on themselves. She tried to acknowledge me with her eyes, but even that seemed to be a strain. I sat beside her for a while, uncertain how you visit someone who can't speak. She didn't want small talk, and I didn't know how to initiate a one-sided conversation about death and dying. So I just sat, feeling young and foolish.

At last I heard a sound. She was looking at me. I leaned closer. She breathed some words. I couldn't make them out. I concentrated as she tried again, but I still couldn't get it. I apologized to her. Then she mouthed very distinctly, "The Lord's my shepherd." I smiled with recognition.

I took her hand and began reciting the lines I thought were indelibly written in my memory. "The Lord is my shepherd. I shall not want. He makes me lie down in green pastures, and leads me beside still waters. He revives my soul. And leads me, and leads me beside still waters. He makes me lie down ..." I was getting dizzy. "He makes ..." I withdrew my hand, frantically trying to remember how it went.

Then I felt the touch of her withered fingers on my arm. "He leadeth me in paths of righteousness," she whispered, her eyes beaming, "even for his own name's sake." Then she recited the whole damn thing. "Even though I walk through the valley of the shadow of death, I fear no evil; for thou art with me; thy rod and thy staff, they comfort me. Thou preparest a table before me in the presence of my enemies; thou anointest my head with oil, my cup overflows. Surely goodness and mercy shall follow me all the days of my life; and I shall dwell in the house of the Lord for ever." The whole time she never took her eyes off me.

For years I couldn't tell that story. My pride prevented it. I thought it was a story about me and about failing. Then, slowly, I came to realize it wasn't about me at all. It was about grace, extravagant grace, overflowing and abundant grace, poured over my head, running down. Like tears, it tasted good in my mouth. And stuck to my ribs.

Gravity

The Ash Wednesday services are over for another year. We have descended into the season of Lent, the season of lamentation, of wailing and the gnashing of teeth, the season of remembering who we really are. No other season gets to the heart of the matter quite like Lent.

This year Trudy, our student assistant, talked me into letting her update the symbol of ashes with something moderns could better relate to. Ours is, after all, a suburban congregation, anxious to own a piece of whatever's current. It seems that what is current these days — in academic circles, at least — does not include the concept of sin.

The real meaning of Ash Wednesday, she argued, is that within our basic human condition of mortality and frailty are hidden the seeds of our divinity, seeds that produce flowers and fruit, seeds of pregnant possiblity that are the very antithesis of the lifelessness we behold in ashes. The word *human*, she reminded me, shares the same root with the word *humus*, that organic matter made from the decomposition of living stuff from which new organisms are given life.

This did seem to make a certain amount of sense. It anticipated the death and resurrection connection of Holy Week, to which Lent points, and promoted a more hopeful view of the human condition. But then, I have been out of school for a while now and find myself a bit overwhelmed by abstract thought. I didn't want to appear out of touch.

So Trudy preached about the soil from which we come. We are dust from the ground, she said, into which God breathes life. We are compost, rich with potential. We are dirt in which God has planted a divine seed. It was not a bad sermon, and really quite fascinating in its own way.

I then invited the congregation to observe a holy Lent and called them forth to receive the sign of "ashes," an ancient sign denoting our human frailty and sinfulness. Forward they came in a line up the centre aisle, kneeling reverently before me, as one by one I anointed their foreheads with potting soil, pinched between my thumb and fingers from a clay flower pot held by Trudy. "Remember you are dirt," I intoned, "and to dirt you shall return." The dirt fell in clumps onto their noses, sprinkling down over their white shirts and blouses.

But I hear things went smoothly for Father David this year, back in my old parish of St. Jude's. Of course, things could only improve year by year from his first Ash Wednesday there. Each Lent since then has represented a kind of rising from the ashes of his own frail humanity.

Father David is a bit of a purist when it comes to liturgy. This does not mean he is a traditionalist; quite the opposite, in fact. He could not afford to be a traditionalist, in any case. Beverley, his wife, with her boundless enthusiasm, leading the startled congregation in sing-along folk-songs, her guitar strings buzzing, her bountiful hips swaying, leaves no room for him to be stuffy.

But he does insist that worship be intentional — even their dated sixties-style folk mass — that it be well thought-out and principled. Father David is nothing if not a man of principle.

There are limits to principles, however. They are fine in the high billowy realms of theory. But brought down to the muck of everyday living, principles are inclined to slip and slide around like the rest of us. This was a lesson that had not been available to Father David when he served his curacy at the cathedral.

There, disconnected from grass roots in the usual sense, and hoisted up instead by a congregation of prominent VIPs who expected their worship to be lavish and grandiose, the clergy swished about in their cassocks doing pretty much as they pleased.

Father David was in his element at the cathedral. The magnificent pipe organ would sound a brassy fanfare as the clergy moved in procession down the long aisle. The paid choir offered complex canticles and titillating motets on behalf of the worshippers. The incense wafted up through shafts of tinted light toward the high vaulted ceilings. This was worship as God intended it, exultant and full-bodied.

It was an intimidating environment for others, though. Even the highly paid wedding consultants and funeral directors instinctively knew their place. They "floated suggestions" or "presented an alternative view," but the final say belonged to the clergy, a responsibility that extended even to young Father David.

So it was difficult for Father David when he first arrived at St. Jude's. Mr. Gavel of the Oldham and Gavel Funeral Home told him that this was simply the way they did things here. Father David looked at Mr. Gavel as if the man were speaking in a foreign language. "Excuse me?" he said.

"Well, you can't have a burial in the winter; the ground's too hard. And you can't do a public interment in the spring because of the run-off. And you can't wait until the summer because there would be a stench. So the vault is the way we do it, always have with every minister before. You wait for a good day and then move the casket out of the vault and into the plot. The families don't usually want to be there. It's just the way it's done here."

"Well, I don't think so," Father David replied evenly. "People need to attend to every step of the grieving process or they don't move through it. And that includes being present at the interment. Now, that's my understanding, and I am after all the rector of this parish."

So Eva Norstrum's interment became an occasion of considerable public interest, more interest, in fact, than she had ever garnered while living. She was a spinster who had lived all her life in the family home, tending her crotchety father well into his old age and far past her own prime. She was a nervous person and people felt a little sorry for her, cooped up there with the old man until he died, only six years before her own death.

But posthumously she became the subject of several sermons as Father David hammered home the point that, having gathered around the font at her baptism, the church had an obligation to be present at her interment, especially as Eva had no known living relatives.

The church, he said, had given far too much away to secular institutions and needed to reclaim its central role at the crossroads of life. Like death, for instance, where grieving had been given up to paid professionals who, after all, were running a business. Taped music, electronic curtains, fashionable limousines (none of which the people of this town had ever seen) — what did these have to do with Christian burial, he asked.

So they would have the opportunity next week, on Ash Wednesday, to reclaim the burial rite. Eva Norstrum's remains would be removed from the vault beneath the church and taken to their final resting place in the church cemetery. He certainly expected the congregation to be present.

Wayne, the rector's warden, took Father David aside and tried to reason with him. "Look," he said in as friendly yet firm a manner as he could, "you're new here. You have to let people do things their own way. Lloyd charges double for digging a grave in the winter on account of the wear and tear on his back-hoe. And if we should get some warm weather like they're calling for and there's run-off, well, the cemetery's not the place you want to be."

But Father David stuck to his guns. Eva would not be denied a proper Christian burial. And besides, Ash Wednesday would be an ideal time for the parish to be reminded of its mortality. Even Beverley held her tongue. Her husband had a right to establish himself as the rector of his parish, even if his obstinacy did seem to be a little extreme.

So Father David drew upon his prerogative as liturgical officer of the parish and combined the Ash Wednesday service with the service of interment. Every detail was thought through and meticulously planned. The service would begin in the church with the readings and sermon. Then the congregation would move in procession to the cemetery that adjoined the church to the east. Mrs. Goode would remain at the organ, so that while the congregation processed out of doors they would hear the music and be reminded that they were still engaged in worship. They would then return solemnly to the church to receive the imposition of ashes.

Father David was feeling quite pleased with himself when the day came. He was already thinking of writing up the service and submitting it to *By What Rite*, a quarterly journal for modern liturgical reformers. When Wayne called at breakfast time to draw his attention to the unseasonable thaw that was causing quite a run-off, Father David simply thanked him for his concern and said he would see him later at the service.

At 10:45 Father David stepped from the rectory and made his way across the street to the church. It was an uncommonly spring-like day. Birds chirped from the overgrown lilac bushes at the edge of the driveway and dropped greetings from the telephone wires overhead. At the road a small river, gurgling wildly, rushed past his feet toward the storm sewer traps farther down the hill. He sucked in the fresh country air and noted with satisfaction that all seemed in readiness for the service.

Two Oldham and Gavel part-timers stood outside the vault door, ready to assist in the removal of the coffin when the time came. Norm greeted Father David in the narthex and offered him a pew bulletin and a hymn book, something he did by force of habit, even though Father David typed the order of service himself and always used his own copy of the hymn book, a special music edition.

Mr. Gavel was seated in the back row of the church and gave Father David a slight nod as he entered. Mrs. Goode was getting ready at the organ, flipping through her music book and pressing the pages open at the right spots. Father David went up into the vestry and robed, feeling triumphant.

At 10:55 he emerged from the vestry in his cassock and surplus — an appropriately sombre choice, he thought — and knelt reverently at the prayer desk to say his prayers. The church was beginning to fill. At 11:00 Norm tolled the bell and Father David got up, kissed his stole, put it round his neck, and made his way down the aisle to join the choir, which had gathered at the back. Mrs. Goode looked up to see that all was ready and then launched into the processional hymn, "Forty Days and Forty Nights." The congregation rose and the service began.

During the sermon Father David laid the foundations for what was to follow. In a few minutes they would be going out to commit Eva's body to the ground. This is all we are, without God. We are dust, and to dust we shall return. Yet they would do so joyfully because they knew that Eva's soul resides with God, eternally. This is God's gift. And so we must all remember, at this the gateway to our Lenten observance: without God we are nothing; with God we have eternal life.

I wish I had had such confidence in my own early days as a preacher. I certainly had never offered the people of St. Jude's such authoritative teaching while I was their young rector. So I can understand with envy that Father David felt a certain sense of pride in the proceedings. Everything was going just as he had planned; he was making his mark in their midst.

He donned his funeral cape and led his flock out the main doors and around the side of the church to the vault. There the two Oldham and Gavel part-timers were joined by four men of the congregation as they entered the vault and emerged with the coffin containing Eva Norstrum. The mud at the entrance sucked at their overshoes and their feet slipped, but they were able to make it up the slight incline to where the snow lay melting in dirty mounds.

They proceeded up the narrow path that had been cleared to Eva's grave. Above the whistle of the wind in the trees and the screech of the transport trucks gearing down as they entered town, they could hear Mrs. Goode at the organ back in the church. They could also hear the sound of water trickling.

When they got to the grave it was already half-filled with water. Mr. Gavel looked anxiously over at Father David. But Father David, calm and self-possessed, assumed his place at the head of the grave while the pallbearers manoeuvred the coffin onto the planks that were extended across the hole. "All of us go down to the dust," Father David read, "yet even at the grave we make our song: alleluia, alleluia, alleluia."

The pallbearers reached for the straps that were laid out beneath the coffin and, lifting it slightly, removed the planks and began lowering the coffin into the grave. A few feet down it slapped the surface of the water and came to rest, bobbing slightly.

Father David was just about to pronounce the blessing when suddenly he dropped out of sight. The ground gave way beneath his feet and down he went into the hole. With three mighty thuds he hit the coffin, first with his heels, then with his tailbone, and then with the back of his head. He lay there stiffly for a moment, trying not to move, his eyes fixed straight ahead, his hands at his sides feeling out the seriousness of his position. But the coffin was tossing as if at sea, and he slid off sideways into the muck. Rolling over, he scrambled to keep from slipping into the watery depths beneath the coffin, then he found the handles and held on.

When he had stabilized his position, wedged lengthwise between the coffin and the dirt wall, half submerged in the watery grave, he looked up into a ring of horrified faces peering down. From the throng a hand emerged from a dark sleeve. Wrapped around it was one end of a strap. Father David reached up and caught hold of the end that was dangling like a lifeline above him and was pulled up into the arms of Mr. Gavel. Off in the distance Mrs. Goode swelled the strains of "Abide with Me."

Father David was sick the following Sunday and a replacement had to be called in for the services. Around three in the afternoon Mrs. Bunting came by with a chicken casserole, and Wayne phoned to see how Father David was getting along. Fine,

Beverley told them, it was just a bug and she was sure he would be back on his feet in no time.

The next morning Mr. Gavel dropped by and asked if Father David was receiving visitors. Beverley knocked softly on the study door, then let him in. Father David was sunk deep in his high backed wing-chair, a book closed on his lap.

"So," Mr. Gavel said with a smile as he took a seat opposite Father David, "how do you want to do things next year?"

The Rise and Fall
of Arthur Pitfield

PITFIELD, The Right Reverend Arthur Dudley-
Suddenly and unexpectedly Wednesday, August 30,
1995, in his 61st year. Recently elected Anglican bishop,
beloved husband of Effy Bown, father of Dr. Sally
Tremblay, David Pitfield, and The Reverend Robert
"Bobby" Pitfield. Friends will be received at Christ
Church Cathedral, Friday, 2–4 p.m. Funeral service
Saturday at 1 p.m. He will be sodly missed.

It was an understated announcement for a public figure. Perhaps that was because the rest of the page was taken up with the
obituary for Yappy Goldfarb, written from the files of no less
than four staff writers.

Yappy, in his ninety-second year, had played baseball for the
Maple Leafs back in the twenties and had lived on as a minor but
beloved icon of that bygone era. His death inspired several pieces
about the modern commercialization of baseball, the relative price
of everyday things then and now, and the loss of innocence in
our present age.

Arthur Pitfield's death, by comparison, must have proved something of a conundrum for the obituary reporters. He was a bishop in the Anglican Church of Canada, a man of unknown public significance, who had been on the job a mere six months. The funeral home that placed the notice could not provide much more, certainly not the details surrounding his recent election. Even so, there are those of us who will miss him — even sodly.

An unremarkable — but also unsullied — career had brought Arthur Pitfield from military chaplaincy to a string of quiet ministries in unassuming parishes. He had sat on many diocesan boards and committees, chairing none, and was not known to hold any particular points of view. He was generally well liked by his parishioners, perhaps because he avoided conflict and simply let the murky waters of parish politics find their own levels.

Nor did he exhibit the least ambition in his ministry. Any personal pride he might have had in his own success he deflected, referring to the wondrous workings of the Spirit and to the constant love and support of the members of his family.

Sally, his oldest, strong and sharp-tongued, is a veterinarian who bought into a thriving practice back in the rolling countryside of Prince Edward County, where the family lived when she was a child. David is a struggling songwriter somewhere in the city. If he never makes a dollar, his charm and idealism still will carry him far, especially into the hearts of his parents.

Bobby, the youngest, followed his father into the ministry. It is clear to any who know him that he regards priesthood as little more than a paid opportunity to pursue his hobbies, which include computer programming and composing songs on his digital keyboard, between the obligatory church meetings and worship services. But he is an engaging preacher nonetheless, who preaches effortlessly without notes, if sometimes also without a clear point.

Arthur loved them all, and doted on their achievements. But it was Effy, their mother, who earned his deepest admiration. The backbone of the family, Effy managed the household on the shoestring budget Arthur's meagre salary allowed, keeping heart and soul together for them all as she marshalled the children through their school years.

People in the parishes Arthur has served have described Effy as a "brick." She was the first to deliver a casserole, or organize a tea, or help out with the Christmas pageant. She thought nothing of advising wayward altar guilds how it was her husband wanted things done, though, in truth, his ideas were not nearly as well formed as her own. Some people even have suggested — and not unkindly — that Arthur's ministry belonged at least half to her.

Arthur met Effy during his student internship on Newfoundland's north-eastern shores. He had seven congregations that summer, five of them outports he could reach only by boat, and only in good weather. He was a skinny young man in outsized robes, and the parish enfolded him to its breast. Every Saturday evening he spent with Effy's family, her mother being churchwarden, and they fattened him up with fish 'n' brewis and tales of their long family history on the sea. Laughter came easily and the colour rose in his cheeks.

I guess it was inevitable that Arthur should marry their eldest daughter and take her away with him to start his ministry on the mainland. There at his side through thirty-two years she has been, quite simply, his whole world, though she would brush off with a laugh his attempts to tell her so.

So no one was more surprised at his election to the episcopate than Arthur himself. His name had not been on the original slate. He was not a dark horse; he was not even in the race. But these are strange times in the church, God moving in mysterious ways. And so it was that Arthur came out of nowhere, right up the middle between the fundamentalist Right and the fundamentalist Left.

The Right was represented by The Reverend Douglas Lawes, a charismatic personality and popular preacher whose "Back to the Bible" newsletter is received into the homes and hearts of hundreds of disgruntled Anglican evangelicals.

For too long, his editorials say, bleeding-heart liberals have compromised the essentials of the faith and weakened the moral fibre of the church. The "liberal captivity" of the church, he has said, has produced the virtual dethronement of Jesus as the second person of the Trinity. In his place now stands Sophia, a goddess figure from the spurious non-canonical Wisdom tradition. As a result men have become soft, abrogating their role as head of the home and turning the church over to women and homosexuals. Only a Spirit-led Bible-based revival, he says, will save God's people from being given up to their base minds and improper conduct, spewed out of the Saviour's mouth, as it says right there in the third chapter of the Book of Revelation.

The Left was represented by The Reverend Canon Holly Wright, an outspoken advocate of the ordination of gays, the de-marginalization of the poor, the feminization of the church, and the democratization of the world. She has chaired just about every committee of the diocese from her position as canon pastor of the cathedral, people often confusing her with the dean, whose name they can never quite call to mind.

Around Holly has formed a network of support groups, people at odds with the church, who meet to share their pain and to work toward social justice and personal wholeness. Some admit openly that the church is already dead and look for inspiration beyond Scripture, beyond Tradition, beyond Reason to Jungian analysis, Celtic roots, and North American native spirituality.

One such follower, Bill Meyers, a diocesan priest and self-proclaimed male feminist, got himself thrown in jail up north last summer by joining his native "sisters and brothers" at a barricade and lying on the road before the police cruisers. He was the only one arrested; the native band never quite figured out who he was or, afterwards, where he had gone.

The synodical electorate had a tough choice. Both candidates had considerable followings, careening off as they did in polar opposite directions. In between was the predictable assemblage of nice middle-aged guys and matronly women nominated by their parish representatives, each hopeful that his, or her, turn had come. In support of one of these candidates, a churchwarden circulated a letter to all synod delegates extolling his rector's particular virtues — his administrative competence, his pastoral skills (cultivated, the letter implied, by his three failed marriages), and his high-ranking position in the Masonic Order. Some believe this hurt him badly.

It was the longest electoral synod in diocesan history. It began with a eucharist on Saturday morning, the metropolitan archbishop presiding but declining to preach, with tensions running so high. After ten hours and thirteen ballots, the archbishop adjourned synod for the day, charging all members to return the next afternoon after deep prayer and serious consideration of the church's future.

Never had so many ballots revealed so little about the mind of the Holy Spirit. An election required a simple majority from the two voting houses of the clergy and laity. But the assembly was split three ways: the Right laity listing toward Lawes, the Left toward Wright, and the rest trading back and forth between the candidates in the middle. The most one could discern was that the Spirit was guiding no one to give up any ground.

The overnight hiatus provided for a flurry of phone calls and hushed meetings as delegates and candidates alike sought new alliances that might break the deadlock. That was when Arthur Pitfield's name was first mentioned, floating tentatively. But then, to everyone's amazement, it began attracting serious attention. He was, all things considered, safe.

So the next day synod members were handed a new slate. A few names had been withdrawn and now Arthur's name appeared, fresh and alphabetically situated smack in the middle of the list. It was a sign, a portent, a way out. It took the synod only two ballots to try on the new fit and make its decision.

The applause was perfunctory as Arthur made his way to the front of the cathedral. As he took the microphone from the archbishop to utter his first words as bishop-elect, synod members were already rising to put on their coats to get home for supper.

The early days were not easy for the new bishop. They started with all the cheap word-plays one might expect of a church dazed and a bit embarrassed by its own actions. The election was described as "pitiful," the new playing field as a "pitfield," the bishop himself as, well, "the pits." In clericus meetings clergy eyed one another as they mentioned his name, trying to read the emerging consensus. It would not be long before they would be making "Where's Arthur?" jokes, after the manner of the "Where's Waldo?" picture book series.

Problems in the diocese, which had been put on back-burners during the election, now leapt out at Arthur like angry flames. Every day fresh disasters crossed his desk: an accusation of sexual abuse against a respected member of the clergy; a threatened lawsuit by a parish being prepared for closure; a financial crisis at Church House itself demanding an urgent review of all diocesan staff positions. Arthur knit his brow and consulted earnestly with his executive archdeacon. But he seemed strangely untouched by it all, as if nothing he could do would, in itself, make the slightest bit of difference.

A few months ago Arthur came to our parish for a service of confirmation. It was my first close-up look at this quiet harmless man who had become my overseer, my boss. I had asked in my letter that he give a children's talk at the start of the service. His secretary said she was sure he would like that.

As we entered the church to the processional hymn, Arthur looked curiously small and round in the cope, which rose from his shoulders to a height behind his head. His ears protruded from under the weight of the mitre.

Arthur didn't have a children's talk prepared. But he sat down with them anyway on the chancel steps. They sat around him, waiting for something to happen, jostling for position, my own children shoving one another back and forth. Playfully he reached out with the staff and caught one around the neck. "That's what it's for, you know," he said, chuckling. A mild joke.

Some of the children pressed in close, speaking in low intimate voices. He leaned forward toward them, answering in whispers. This was not like the children's talks the congregation was used to. He felt no compulsion to announce loudly for the amusement of the rest of us the private revelations of children not yet prepossessed enough to play to the crowd themselves. He was having, quite literally, a talk with the children. After it was over they filed out the side door with their Sunday school teachers.

Arthur lingered for a moment. I looked down at him from my place at the prayer desk. No one in the congregation appeared to carry less authority than this small man sitting atop my chancel steps. He watched the last of the children head toward their classrooms for colouring and flannel board stories and paper cut-outs; it was almost as if he wished he could go with them.

Last Wednesday Arthur was making his way from his office on the third floor down the back stairway to a service of institution in the chapel. Two priests were waiting to receive their formal commissioning to their new ministries — ministries that were "mine and thine," Arthur would be reminding them in the brief service. But, as often happens when men try to wear long robes, Arthur stepped on his hem and walked up into his alb, hurtling headlong down the second flight.

He was shaken but okay, he said, when he emerged in the chapel, a trickle of blood running down his forehead. But just into the service, with the priests kneeling before him, he grew disoriented. He rocked for a moment on his heels, and then fell over backward into the altar, slumping to the sanctuary floor.

It has taken precisely no time at all for the power brokers to begin planning for Arthur's successor. At his funeral word was being whispered around that Jim Hovey was thinking of returning to the diocese and would likely let his name stand. A respected professor of ethics and a well-known modern interpreter of the Anglican *via media*, Jim's name has generated much hushed excitement.

But I couldn't think too much about that. I am caught instead by the image of Arthur sitting on the chancel steps watching the children make their way to Sunday school. I can't really say I knew the man. But I think I now have an inkling how the innkeeper must have felt that cold Christmas night so long ago. And what it's like to miss the moment when it comes.

Mr. Briggs
Goes to Church

Being open-minded has its limits. They say you can be so open-minded your brains fall out. They must have been thinking of some of the clergy I know.

Why else would we feel compelled to take seriously every idea that floats past our open minds like so many dust particles? It's as if at ordination we are ontologically changed indeed, losing any capacity to judge between good ideas and bad, becoming benign guardians of the mediocre, the novel-for-novelty's-sake, and the just plain dumb.

Bright ideas come across my desk routinely in attractively designed packages. Accompanied by music booklets and suggestions for supplementary crafts and children's activities, these packages are responsible for the felling of entire forests, only to end up filling both a recycling container *and* a good-sized waste-paper basket in my office.

Fortunately, decision making about all these bright ideas is actually made easier by their sheer volume. I linger only over those that have my name typed, or handwritten, on the envelope — *not* those that have been electronically reproduced from a computer list. And the ones marked "To the Pastor," or worse, "To the Reverend" — those don't get even a second glance.

Opening a package from Church House, bulging with good ideas for ministry, is a particularly bad idea. I lost my head not long ago and found myself sifting through an assortment of liturgical resources for saints' days and other feasts of the church. I was amazed to think that people actually get paid to write this sort of stuff.

There was a musical mass for St. Cecilia's Day entitled, "Make a Joyful Noise." It featured a setting for organ, choir, and noise-makers — the idea being that the solemn tones of the organ would intermittently be brightened by the choir breaking into a chorus of, "Dip, dip, do, dip," and by the congregation playing kazoos and party whistles.

A children's liturgy for the Conversion of St. Paul featured a glass communion "beaker" that — presto! — turns water to wine, or at least to a wine-coloured liquid that is drinkable. In God's good providence things are not what they seem at first and can, in fact, become something even better. Like the apostle himself, I guess, was the point.

I once thought a Bible on a lectern, bread and wine on the table, a few people in the pews — these simple elements might actually be enough. But no, it seems we have to add spectacle — properly advertised and reported in the local paper, of course — and so turn sacred worship into a three-ring circus.

A colleague gushed to me recently about the "Welcome Back Sunday" he did in his parish last September. First he had the congregation gather in the church hall instead of the church. The startled parishioners heard some readings and then were invited to play with a huge parachute, everyone holding on to an edge as it wafted up and down. Each time it rose various combinations of church members scrambled to exchange places beneath the billowing tent as their young rector called out, "Everyone wearing blue socks!" or "If you had corn flakes for breakfast!"

This is worship?

I am liberal enough in these matters — and, I guess, politically astute enough — to have a functioning worship committee in my own parish. We meet monthly to read books and articles, to discuss new developments in the field, and to set a general course for the worship here. I have made sure there is an equal number of traditionalists and modernists, so that nothing too wild is likely to happen on a Sunday morning.

But at our last meeting someone reported on the cathedral's recent "Blessing of the Animals" service. They brought the clipping from the diocesan newspaper. To illustrate the thrust of the story there was a photograph of a dog, an old basset hound, looking uncertain, its ears drooping over the proud hands of the child who held it. A smiling priest, Holly Wright, an advocate of this sort of thing, was reaching out toward the pet, her hand in the sign of a blessing. Another child off to the side could be seen giggling.

We passed the article around. People perked up. It made the church seem so, I don't know, friendly, someone said. The others nodded. We're not as stodgy as people think, after all. And there has been a great deal of research lately into the therapeutic role of pets, someone else suggested. They give cats to seniors, don't they, for company? And bunny rabbits to prison inmates, to teach

them how to care for something. And pet cemeteries are becoming big business, someone added.

I could see where this was leading. But before I could figure out how to cut them off at the pass, the room fell silent. Everyone was looking at me. What did I think?

The truth is, I hate this stuff! The diocesan paper is filled each month with just such cheesy exhibitionism, photos of grown adults standing around grinning sheepishly, some poor child held upside down by his ankles as the bishop "beats the bounds" of the parish, all for the sheer fun of it. Are we so bored with the basic faith that has been handed down to us that we are driven to this? Where is Oliver Cromwell when you need him?

Though, admittedly, there was something sort of touching about this particular picture, the old dog's sad eyes, its eyebrows raised toward the hand that is blessing it. What was it feeling, one had to wonder, in this its fleeting moment of fame? Was it in some doggy way enjoying the limelight? Was its little heart pounding with pride and excitement? Or was it simply tolerating the fuss until it could return to its well-worn rug by the kitchen door? How would you know?

All right, all right, I finally conceded. The Feast of St. Francis of Assisi was coming up, and if we wanted, we could do something on a Sunday afternoon. But nothing stupid. No horses or cows. No pythons or lizards. Just your ordinary house pets, cats and dogs, that sort of thing. And there wouldn't be communion. I didn't want to have to deal with *that* question.

Someone suggested we have a reception to follow, and perhaps some sort of pageant with prizes for the Most Lovable Pet, or the Least Likely Pet. I quickly countered that animals, like people, were all equal before God and we should not be singling any out. If we were going to have a reception, tea and dog biscuits would be sufficient.

It became apparent in the weeks that followed that the worship committee had its finger on the pulse of the community, and not merely the church community. Strangers began calling to find out if they had to be Anglican to come, meaning presumably the pet owners, not the pets. The service was proving to be popular before it even happened.

When the day came, the place was abuzz with activity. I arrived to find the sidespeople spreading newspapers down the side aisles. Someone had thoughtfully placed boxes with kitty litter in the corners. A huge banner, printed on computer paper, had been hung around the narthex, quoting the Apocryphal Prayer of Azariah: "Bless the Lord, you whales and all that swim in the waters" (God forbid!); "Bless the Lord, all birds of the air" (in cages, maybe); "Bless the Lord, all wild animals and cattle" (I said no cows): "Sing praises to him and highly exalt him forever."

The pew bulletin had been made up by Grace, our church secretary, on her own time. It featured a picture of Noah's ark, and a verse from Genesis: "Out of the ground the Lord God formed every animal of the field and every bird of the air, and brought them to the man to see what he would name them." Grace herself was bringing her shih-tzu, whom she had named Mitsy.

And then the congregation began to arrive: gerbils in cages on their treadmills; German shepherds held in check by choke chains; an ant colony working right up to the last minute between plates of glass; a rat named Rufus; a nervous armadillo on a leash; felines of every size and colour, some with rhinestone flea-repellent collars. In they came, two by two, anxious to be there, anxious to be anywhere, dragging their owners behind them.

The church provided a marvellous new world for them, filled as it was with species and breeds they had only ever dreamed of, or perhaps seen on television commercials, and then only in two dimensions. The dogs sniffed at the cats, the cats hissed and swatted at the dogs, the armadillo hid beneath a pew, birds chirped and squawked in their cages, eyed by the cats.

As the noise level approached that of the Christmas Eve children's service, I went up to Barry, our organist, and whispered, "We'd better get this show on the road!" He stepped on the volume pedal and we launched into the processional hymn, "For the Beauty of the Earth," to which Barry had added a verse of his own:

For the creatures thou hast made,
for the pets that grace our homes,
for each bark, each mew, each bray
— comfort when we feel alone:
Lord of all to Thee we raise
this our grateful hymn of praise.

The congregation, comprised of as many new faces as familiar ones, endured the readings and the little homily I tried to deliver above the din. Leashes were shortened, bristling fur coats were smoothed, sharp words were whispered. Then the sidespeople moved forward and the blessings began.

The two German shepherds, Tyrone and Guthrie, must have thought my outstretched hand to mean some sort of military command. They began barking wildly, rearing up on their hind legs, straining at their leashes, their slobber falling in foamy white clots on the carpet. I tried to remain calm as I lowered my hand and backed away.

A tabby kitten named Mineu was oblivious to the uproar. I squatted to receive her at the chancel steps. She crawled up into the lap of my alb, then settled down for a little nap as she received her blessing.

The gerbils seemed particularly indifferent to being blessed, nosing nervously around the little poops and the shredded paper lining the bottom of their cage. Roger the Armadillo seemed more concerned about shrinking away from the public eye.

Fritz, a mean-looking overstuffed grey Persian, became ornery when placed before me and tried to bite the hand that blessed it. Breaking free, he shook me off, preened a little, and then began roaming at will behind my back in the sanctuary.

The line moved forward up the centre aisle. It was odd, but I found I was enjoying myself. There was no use being excessively formal, though I had memorized a standard blessing to use for all the pets. I learned each one's name from the owner and then extended a hand, or took it into my arms as seemed prudent, and had a "moment" with each. The owners themselves glowed with pride.

Finally, at the end of the line, five-year-old Lucy Turcot came forward with her green budgie in a domed cage, like Tweetie Bird's. Lucy's mom accompanied her, bending over watchfully as Lucy presented the cage to me. I knelt down and asked the budgie's name. "Mr. Briggs," Lucy said. She explained how everyday she put seed in his feeder and water in his little dish. Sometimes her parents let her take him out and his tiny feet would wrap themselves around her fingers.

I raised my hand to give the blessing. "Mr. Briggs," I began, "God's richest blessing upon you and your kind ..." (something was moving off to my left) "... whose life and witness ..."

From behind the potted palms Fritz the Persian seized the moment and sprang forward, a grey streak leaping three feet through the air. People gasped. Fritz was focused on Mr. Briggs, not on the cage that held him, so his face ricocheted off the door with a loud clang, knocking the cage out of Lucy's hand and sending it rolling down the aisle. The startled cat, dazed by the blow, darted off in the other direction, shaking his head violently as he went.

Lucy's mom quickly moved forward and uprighted the cage. Mr. Briggs lay motionless on the bottom. Lucy looked on in horror. "Oh, no. Oh, no," her mom started saying. "It's all right, Lucy, darling, it's all right." Lucy looked at me, confused.

I opened the cage door and reached in. Tentatively I touched the little bird. If it was not dead, it was pretty close to it. I picked it up. I had never held a bird before. Its feathers felt smooth against the palm of my hand. Lucy reached her hand in and stroked the soft down of its breast with her finger. "Mr. Briggs?" she said. Her mother put her hand to her mouth, her eyes brimming with tears.

But wait. Was that a little movement in his chest? I put my thumb over the spot. (How does one take the pulse of a bird?) Did I just feel him stir? Mr. Briggs opened his eyes and blinked once, then again. And then, with a flutter, he was lifted and gone, out of the cage and circling high overhead. Lucy's mom hugged her daughter to her. "He's alive!" she cried. "Mr. Briggs is alive, Lucy!" The congregation, which had risen to its feet, broke into spontaneous applause. Children squealed. Dogs began barking.

It was a magnificent climax to the service, though it took about an hour and a half to get Mr. Briggs down and safely stowed in his cage again. Fritz the Persian was caught by his owner and led away in shame.

The local newspaper came out the next day with a picture of me on the front page, kneeling low beside Lucy with Mr. Briggs in the palm of my hand. "Budgie Raised from Dead," the headline announced. I had to smile. It had not been such a bad idea, after all. At least we had had an open mind.

Bud Blakelock's Bequest

I learned of Bud Blakelock's death the day Quebec almost walked out on Canada. The two events, so far removed from each another, haunt me still. They both point in the same direction: to the senseless pain of separation, and to what remains when you try to divide that which is indivisible.

Growing up in Quebec, I had observed the ways that lead to separation, though "political independence," "sovereignty association" — these were not phrases we commonly heard or used. I came into my teens in Montreal's West Island, which in the sixties was a kind of English suburban ghetto. We knew Quebec was a French-speaking province, but we lived within a self-contained universe that rarely forced us to admit it.

Every morning I delivered seventy-nine copies of the *Montreal Gazette* to my English-reading neighbours. Then I rode on a school bus filled with my English-speaking friends and made small trouble all day at my English-language public high school. On Saturday nights I played in an English-singing rock band (when the words could be heard at all), and on Sunday mornings I attended an Anglican church where we prayed in the proper language of King James, the language spoken by Jesus himself.

When our high school band took the occasional field trip downtown to the Place des Arts for a matinée performance of the Montreal Symphony Orchestra, my friend Dave and I snuck out from the line-up and made our way instead down French streets, past French shops and bistros, to the English-speaking pawnshops on Craig Street, to Golden Imports and the original Steve's Music Store. There we hung off the street-smart banter of the bullshit artists who ran the shops, haggling our way into manhood New York-style.

French language and culture existed hazily somewhere just beyond our close-focused adolescent field of vision: incoherent clowns overdressed and overacting on French television; reports of sold-out concerts downtown featuring popular Quebecois bands with names we never bothered to learn; jean- and leather-clad bikers lounging in front of a local watering hole, whose taunts and insults we didn't have to take seriously because they were tossed at us, as we passed by, in French. Ours was an English world.

Our parents could feel it, though, the turbulent waters rising to the very gunwales of our genteel English punt. That's why we moved. French salesclerks were becoming uppity, and the St. Jean Baptiste Day marches downtown were growing more violent every year. Eventually there would be the FLQ, the kidnappings, and the War Measures Act. But we had left by then, and those terrifying days belonged to someone else.

I was brooding about Quebec, my home province, and its most recent tryst with separation from the rest of Canada, when I learned of Bud Blakelock's death, and about his bequest to the church of a stained glass window.

The bequest was expected. The window was to complete a set he had commissioned after his wife, Dorothy, died ten years ago. He had donated the first window to St. Jude's while I was rector there, as a memorial to her. It was installed in the north transept, just to the left of a blank window that retained the sickly greenish wash of opaque sculptured plexiglass. Though it had been completed at the same time, Bud held back the second window, intending to make it a kind of memorial to himself after his own death. One day the two would combine to form a single scene, a striking depiction of the Easter garden.

This second window, by all reports, is a beautiful thing to see. It is an eight-foot-high representation of the empty tomb. The stone has been rolled back to reveal the linen cloths folded neatly inside. The tomb is set in the midst of flowering plants and shrubs, the sun rising on the distant horizon. An inscription below, being of course the second part of the verse, reads, "He is risen."

St. Jude's itself is a staid grey stone church, standing in muted dignity at the east end of town. The original church had been located at the town's centre, right at the main intersection. In 1921, after a fire tore through that quaint wooden structure, the hopeful and forward-thinking congregation decided to enlarge the church and rebuild it east of town, where a railway line was supposed to be coming through.

It was a time of wild optimism, a time when small rural communities, caught up in the spirit of the League of Nations and the New World Order, were taking for themselves names of international import. The neighbouring village of Burns had just renamed itself Utopia, and at the barren unnamed crossroads out by the cemetery a sign suddenly appeared, declaring, "The Village of Peace — established 1919." In that spirit the town considered giving itself a new name and a new image. The town of Continent was a strong contender for a while — "Working as One for a Better World" — until someone rehearsed out loud what it would actually sound like to say they lived in Continent.

The people of St. Jude's felt certain the town would develop to the east, and located the new church strategically at the heart of its future. But the promised railway never came, leaving the new church no choice but to hold its head high in the manner of a cat caught doing something dumb, like falling backward off a couch, as if to say, "That may have *looked* dumb to you, but I knew *exactly* what I was doing. I think I'll just go take a nap now." It was the last progressive idea St. Jude's ever had.

Bud himself was not exactly a progressive thinker. He had been a churchwarden during my time there, and was one of the undisputed patriarchs of the church — and of the town, too, for that matter, which was quite an accomplishment for someone not born there. He "married in," as they say. He had met Dorothy during the war, at the wedding of a friend. As Dorothy had no brothers, Bud came to share in her inheritance of the family farm, which he then turned into one smart operation, winning the respect and admiration of the surrounding farming community.

For a time Bud was reeve of the town and then, just as he was about to retire, he was offered a seat on the Milk Marketing Board. This made Bud a virtual citizen of the world in the eyes of most people. He went off to conferences all over the province, even to a national convention once in Swift Current, Saskatchewan.

Bud's church involvement was on much the same level, an extension of his civic duty. As churchwarden, he pinched pennies and made sure the rector was doing his job, visiting the older folks and that sort of thing. As for church attendance itself, he got himself up and out on Sundays in the same frame of mind with which he had risen early all those dark mornings to milk the cows: it was a necessary chore, though not too unpleasant, so long as the sermon didn't go on forever and everything else remained more or less predictable. Which meant that, sooner or later, Bud was bound to collide with the progressive ideas of Father David.

Father David followed me at St. Jude's, fresh from three years as assistant curate at the cathedral. He was an intense young man who wanted to make his mark in this his first parish by helping this conservative rural congregation enter at least the nineteenth century, if not actually the twentieth.

The people themselves hadn't been too unhappy with things the way they were. But he told them the parish was out of step with changes happening the world over. The church was on the move, he said. Gone were the days when you could walk into an Anglican church anywhere in the world and be welcomed by the *Book of Common Prayer*. If they were to happen into a church in, say, New Zealand or South India or Nigeria, they would be in for a rude awakening — bold new liturgies, contemporary music, concern for social justice.

This was not a thought that had crossed the minds of very many of Father David's parishioners. But no one really wanted to appear so provincial as to state the obvious, that they were not *intending* to happen into a church in one of those foreign places. So they allowed themselves to be browbeaten into using the new green prayer book and having communion every week and singing folk-songs accompanied on the guitar by Father David's wife, Beverley. They took it, but they didn't like it.

One Sunday Father David explained that as Christians we gather for worship not only to make our peace with God but to make our peace with one another as well. So before the collection was to be taken up, they would each turn to their neighbour and exchange the ancient "kiss of peace," which, he explained, in this day and age, could be liberally interpreted as a handshake or some other friendly gesture. The words accompanying this gesture ought to be something like, "The peace of Christ" or "Peace be with you."

Now, Bud knew everyone in that church. He knew their personal problems, how much tax they paid, who had voted for him in that last election, and who hadn't. Frankly, he wasn't coming to church to meet his neighbours. He saw them and saw quite enough of them, thank you very much, every day, including Doris Benchley, who had turned friendly in the last year or so. Nobody — and he meant nobody! — was going to tell him who to talk to in his own church.

The time came in the service for the passing of the peace. It got off to a bad start when Father David asked everyone to turn and greet the person on their immediate right. They all turned and found themselves staring at the back of their neighbour's head, except for the ones at the far right of each row, who turned to face the empty aisle or, on the south side of the nave, to face the wall. After they had sorted things out they began awkwardly shaking hands with one another and mumbling, "Good morning, how are ya?"

But Bud sat back down, folding his arms across his chest, staring straight ahead. Doris Benchley, oozing neighbourliness, turned around from the pew in front of him and reached out her hand. "Good morning, Bud," she said in a sweet singsong voice.

Bud's message in return was pretty clear. He got up, turned around, walked out of the church, and never went back again.

Still, it was a foregone conclusion that, when Bud died, St. Jude's would be the beneficiary of the second window, and that Bud himself would be duly memorialized in the north transept alongside Dorothy, his dearly departed wife.

When the will was read, indeed, the window went to the church. But not to St. Jude's! Damning the winds of change right to the end, Bud had left it to Holy Family Catholic Church, way out on the other side of town, where for some years Father Joe had been lashing out at all things faddish and spiritually lax, things like guitars and folk-songs and tambourines in church — a view obviously shared by Bud. No one could believe it, least of all the folks at Holy Family who, though mystified, were nonetheless glad to receive such a lovely gift.

Quebec did not walk out on the rest of Canada that day. There she stood in the doorway, suitcase in hand, with that determined look of hers. She was well into her "I'm leaving you, we're through" speech, eyes blazing, nostrils flaring, when all of a sudden, by some hair's breadth change of heart, she paused, let go of the bag, and collapsed back on the couch. She had come so close this time.

Meanwhile, the original window now stands alone at the Church of St. Jude, the patron saint of "difficult circumstances," the first panel of a two-window set depicting the Easter garden. There are a few trees in bloom in the background and beyond them some distant rose-coloured hills. In the foreground an angel in radiant white robes sits casually on a large stone, gesturing off-camera to the right, in the direction of the blank window of greenish plexiglass.

Beneath the scene, etched in the glass, is an inscription. It says, simply, "He is not here."

Pulling Up Tares

Jesus was a practical man. Don't hit anybody unless you want to get hit yourself. Settle your arguments before the sun goes down, especially if you're planning to sleep with that person. Don't pull your weeds, they might be rhododendrons.

I wish I'd known some of this when I was part-owner of a lawn care company. "University Gardening Service" was what we had painted on the side of our van. It was meant to increase the benevolence factor. Prospective customers were being asked not merely to have their grass cut, but also to help put a few enterprising young people through college. What we didn't put on that sign, not knowing precisely the difference between a weed and a rhododendron, was our unofficial motto: "If in doubt, yank it out."

The thing I've learned since becoming a homeowner my-self is that you shouldn't start pulling up weeds unless you intend to be at it a very long time. It's a job you never finish. Live and let live, this was Jesus' teaching — sort of — and it still makes a lot of sense today.

Scott, my rector's warden, is one of those people who just can't let a thing be. Last Friday he took some holiday time that was owed him and stayed home to catch up on some minor home repairs. He and his wife, Carolyn, have no children; so their house is pretty tidy most of the time. But because they are both professional people — he's with an insurance company, she sells real estate — they don't spend a lot of time at home, and things tend to get away on them.

In any case, they had invited the parish council over for "wine and savouries" on Sunday afternoon. This provided Scott the motivation to finally get at some of those vexatious signs that their home was acquiring a "lived-in" look.

Scott rose early and got himself organized for the day. He put the tools he thought he'd need in his carpenter's belt — several kinds of screwdrivers, an oil can, a hammer, a small tin of putty and a putty knife, a brown felt-tipped marker, an old rag — and began moving slowly from room to room, like a hunter. He silenced squeaky doors, patched tiny nicks in the plaster, removed scuffs from the quarter-round, touched up gashes in the woodwork.

Midway through the morning, satisfied with his progress so far, he removed his tool belt, made himself a fresh cup of coffee, and took it into the den for a break. He turned on the stereo to catch a few minutes of the CBC, a pleasure denied him in the office environment. He was just lowering himself into the big overstuffed chair when he noticed something he had never seen before.

Beneath the antique lamp table, the one that showed off the Brazilian mahogany lamp, was a stain on the carpet. It was not an obvious stain, more a dark patch on an otherwise monotone taupe expanse. But it was undeniable. He put his coffee down carefully on the side table, on a Club Med coaster depicting sailboats moored off a sandy lagoon, and bent down to examine it.

It was an odd shape, fanning out from an indistinct centre point but with two straight edges that suggested a drink had been spilled with such force that the liquid had shot out of the glass like paint from a gun. He ran his finger over the spot. It had long since dried, leaving no greasy film or hardened edges.

Scott went to the kitchen and dampened a clean tea towel with cool water. He returned and began dabbing at the edges of the stain. This had no effect. He poured a little club soda on the cloth and rubbed at the spot again. He tried a little more, applying it this time directly to the carpet. It bubbled up, hissed, and then dissolved into the carpet's thick pile. Scott continued to dab at it, holding the cloth up intermittently for inspection. The stain yielded nothing.

Downstairs in the laundry room, Scott and Carolyn have an impressive collection of cleaning products, which Scott has organized from left to right according to strength. The window cleaner, a blue spray bottle, was on the far left, with a large plastic refill canister in behind. At the far right was the drain de-clogger, a powerful skull and crossbones concentrate of harmful chemicals that required industrial gloves, a gauze mask, and a well-ventilated room. The gloves and mask were tucked neatly beside the bottle, ready for use.

He reached for the carpet and upholstery cleaner, about midway along the shelf. The directions recommended he test it first on an inconspicuous corner of the material to make sure it wouldn't affect the colour. He was to moisten the area with a misty spray of water, then apply the cleaner from about six inches until it rose in a light foam. He was to let it sit for three minutes, then remove with a damp cloth in light circular motions. DO NOT SCRUB, it warned.

Scott removed the foam with the prescribed light circular motions and inspected the area. It was hard to tell what was moistened carpet and what was stain, so he had to step back. No, it was still there. He rubbed it some more, this time coming dangerously close to scrubbing. Clearly, this was not your superficial stain.

He went off to find the Damp 'n' Dust Buster, the cordless hand-held vacuum that removes both cookie crumbs and lemonade spills with but a quick and easy — click, snap — change of attachments. He found it in its appointed place in the broom closet in the kitchen.

He scoured the area on his hands and knees, pressing the nozzle deep into the carpet. It whirred efficiently as it sucked at the moisture left from the foam and soda water. He could hear tiny objects being inhaled into the removable disposal bag, the common daily jetsam of suburban living, microscopic some of it. When he stood up the blood drained from his head and he had to wait, unsteady for a moment, for the stars to disappear before his eyes. But the stain remained.

He rubbed his chin. It was a good thing he was home today. Otherwise they might not have noticed this until the room was filled with church people. And regardless of how they kept their own homes, he was a churchwarden, and the one with specific responsibility for the building and property. It was more than a matter of personal pride — it was a matter of professional integrity. He was damned if he was going to be beaten by a stubborn stain.

The Rent-A-Way outlet was in a run-down strip plaza that had a variety store, a fish 'n' chips shop, a video arcade, and several graffiti-laden boarded-up premises. Bunk — or was it

Hunk, Scott wondered, as he tried to read the appliquéd script on the manager's shirt pocket — was leaning forward on the counter, blowing smoke into the face of a guy who was haggling for a better deal on a jack-hammer. His shirt sleeves were rolled up high to reveal menacing tattoos on both arms.

Scott wandered away among the tamping machines and chain-saws, the two-stroke post-hole diggers, and the one-man hydraulic lifts. A layer of soot covered everything, and the air hung thick with oil and gasoline. He tried not to touch anything.

There were, it seemed, two models of steam cleaners. One was the Maid O' the Mist "Clean-Bee," a domestic unit like the kind you see for rent in supermarkets. It was cunningly designed with a clear domed cap so you could watch the dirty water swishing around while the hose attachment did its job.

Scott considered this for a moment. It would be $19.99 if he returned it by 5 o'clock that afternoon. But the stain had already proved tenacious. If this unit couldn't do it, he'd be back anyway, $19.99 later, to rent the big industrial cleaner next to it. He may as well just skip that step and go straight for the no-nonsense Acme Industrial Carpet Cleaner at $39.99. And besides, he wasn't sure he wanted to go up to the counter and say to Bunk, or Hunk, "I'd like to rent the Clean-Bee, please."

There was nothing remotely consumer-friendly about the industrial unit. It stood solidly about four feet high, like a gas pump, with no glass bubbles or aerodynamic styling. At one time it had been rocket red but now was scratched and faded beyond any semblance of its original aesthetic. It was supposed to move around on four castors, but the hose was attached at the top in such a way that only a fool would yank it forward and expect the Red Rocket actually to follow without tipping and dumping its dirty contents all over your newly cleaned broadloom. Maybe that was the point, a kind of revolving-door rental scam that meant, try as you might, you would just have to keep coming back.

Still, Scott was hopeful as he struggled to get a grip on the unit from the back of their mini-van. He hugged it to his chest like a bag of cement and brought it to the front door. He was able to prop the door open with his leg and squeeze through. But just as he got inside the unit slipped through his fingers. It crashed onto the floor, its metal wheels sending a large chip of tile flying out toward the boot rack.

"Damn!" Scott muttered. He inspected the damage to the floor. There was a sizeable hole right in the middle of the vestibule, a place your eye naturally fell as you entered the house and bent to take your shoes off. He found the chip. He could probably glue it back, but the repair would be obvious. "Damn!" he said again.

He placed the chip in his pocket and lugged the Rocket up the three steps to the main floor and down the hall past the living-room, through the kitchen, and into the den. The living-room is a room "in process" and, although furnished, is considered by Scott and Carolyn to be too sparse for entertaining. The den, by comparison, is filled with knick-knacks and mementos deliberately chosen and artfully displayed to express something of who they are.

An antique brick fireplace is the defining feature of the den, with its weathered barn beam mantle that Scott purchased at a rural auction. It had been a steal, Scott thought, at $750 and it continues to bring him great satisfaction when guests admire the exposed hand-hewn adze marks.

At the far end of the room is a corner cabinet with interior lighting that highlights some fine lead crystal, a few Royal Doulton pieces, and Carolyn's figurine collection. Closer to the entrance is the sitting nook with its two large stuffed chairs, a compact stereo system hidden amid some old books and hanging ferns on dark oak shelving, and beneath the window the antique table with its exotic lamp. The room is painted a soothing hunter green.

It took six full buckets of water to fill the Rocket's water chamber. The special detergent — which Scott had had to purchase separately —went in another chamber, and then the hose was locked into place on top. At the end of the hose was a large nozzle like the carpet attachment on a vacuum cleaner, only wider. It featured an awkwardly placed trigger that released extra detergent for spot cleaning.

Scott got himself ready, planting his feet firmly apart, nozzle poised in the air. He leaned over and flipped the starter switch. The Acme Industrial Carpet Cleaner roared to life. The floor rumbled, the windows rattled, and the porcelain figurines began to dance and twirl, clinking together inside the corner cabinet.

Scott aimed the nozzle at the stain. Slowly he lowered it to the carpet. As it came within about a foot, the nozzle suddenly lunged at the floor, almost wrenching itself out of his hands. It caught the carpet in a leech's grip and began sucking furiously.

As Scott moved the nozzle over the area the carpet rose up to meet it, as if some small rodent were burrowing its way across the floor. It was only with great effort that he could move it at all — jerk it, really, was all he could do — across the stained area. Back and forth he shoved the heavy nozzle as it growled and grunted, devouring deep dust and floor tacks that hadn't been disturbed since the day the carpet was laid.

Sweat started running down the sides of his face. But the stain remained. His thumb found the detergent trigger and he gave it a shot. The nozzle frothed at the mouth for a moment, making a gasping sound. Scott gave it another shot, and then another, when suddenly he heard the sound of glass smashing.

He whirled around in time to see the door of the corner cabinet swing open and the Royal Doulton terrine come crashing to the floor, where the anniversary champagne glasses had landed only seconds before.

"No!" he cried, extending his arm. He turned back and tried to lift the nozzle from the carpet. It wouldn't let go. He leaned back and pulled until finally the nozzle jerked free, sputtering madly, sending him tumbling into the side table. His morning coffee spun off its coaster, off the limp sails and their languid lagoon, in a dramatic arc to the floor.

Recovering quickly, he lunged for the switch, hit it, and held on to the cleaner with both hands as it rumbled slowly to a halt.

The house fell silent.

He was breathing hard. His hands still clinging to the unit, he surveyed the damage: fragments of crystal and porcelain in the far corner, a potted plant overturned near the door, and a coffee stain now spreading like an oil slick a few feet away.

Then he heard the front door. Carolyn had come home for lunch.

"Scott?" she called out. "Scott, are you home?"

"I'm in here," he answered, trying to control the tremor in his voice.

"Is everything all right, hon? What's happened to the tile here?" She came down the hallway. "Scott? Sco ... what's going ... what have you been doing? What's this thing? Oh, my God, the Royal Doulton ... no, not our anniversary glasses! Scott! What's been going on here?"

Scott let go of the Rocket, straightened himself up and took a deep breath. "I was removing a stain from the carpet," he said.

"Where?" Carolyn demanded. "Where's the stain?"

"Here, by the lamp table. It wouldn't come out."

Carolyn walked directly over to the spot. She lifted the lamp. And as she did, as if by magic, the stain lifted along with it.

"Was that the stain? Scott, was that the stain?"

Scott looked down, horrified. He was overcome with shame. Now, where a dull shadow caused by the overcast morning sky had played tricks with his eyes, a very new, very real stain appeared, lighter than the carpet, bleached as if by the sun. There was nothing he could say.

It made for a funny story on Sunday afternoon, for what else could they do but draw attention themselves to the stain that now dominated the room? But the truth was that, while the champagne glasses and terrine were irreplaceable — one due to sentiment, the other due to expense — the carpet itself now would have to be replaced, and probably the front hall tiles, too. It broke Scott's heart to think of it.

I don't know, but when it comes to weeds, sometimes it's better not even to get started.

The Return of William Trelawny

Today is the Feast of the Baptism of our Lord. To honour the day we had a baptism of our own, though I doubt it bore much resemblance to that event so long ago.

For one thing, the baptizees kept their clothes on. For another, we had people who didn't want to be there, friends and relatives of the candidates who pouted their way through the service as if I were some junior high school teacher making extreme and unusual demands — like that they actually participate in the service. Sullenly they sat or they stood, staring back on me, daring me to come down and ream them out. I was tempted.

In Jesus' day they wouldn't have had it so good. There would not likely have been pews, for instance. Or orders of service with helpful page references and with little cartoon announcements to make it easier for children to follow along. I doubt there would have been greeters, or welcome cards, or friendly opening remarks from John the Baptist, or accommodating photo opportunities round the font afterwards. There was just sun and heat and crowds. There was water, of course, and then the wilderness.

It makes it a little hard to understand why Jesus would have put himself through it. It was not as if he needed a "baptism of repentance for the forgiveness of sins," as the Gospel of Mark describes it. Did his mom push him into it, kind of like confirmation these many years later? "Come on now, Jesus, you've been moping around this house long enough. A little water never hurt anybody. All your friends are going down there. You want to be the only one not baptized?"

Or was it one of those things you do, not because it makes rational sense, but because it feels suddenly necessary, even urgent? Like a groom on his way to the church, who can't resist the urge to drive out one last time past his old childhood home. There he pulls over to the curb, just to sit awhile. He does this only half thinking, as if he is trying to retrieve something, to remember something. Then he takes a deep breath, puts the car in gear, and moves out into the rest of his life.

Anyway, it put me in mind of the return of William Trelawny a few years ago to St. Jude's, the rural parish I served when I was newly ordained and fresh out of college. Father David is there now, of course, and has been since I left.

Father David is the age of the sons and daughters of most of his parishioners, sons and daughters who have grown up and moved away. So "Father" is an honorary title more than a descriptive one. He insists upon it, nonetheless. To their credit, having trained many young clergy over the years, the congregation respects his wishes, but with a knowing smile that makes him feel even younger than he is. How well I recall that smile!

St. Jude's stands in the middle of a forked intersection as you head east out of town, a resolute symbol of the Anglican "middle way." One road takes you northward through rolling countryside past dairy farms and wood lots in a huge loop that eventually leads you out past Holy Family Catholic Church, high atop O'Gorman Hill, and then back into town from the west. The other road takes you southward to the highway and on to the city. This is the route most people seek out.

That year the notice board on the front lawn read, "A Church for Those Who Don't Know Which Way to Turn." I guess these were intended to be words of comfort for out-of-towners who were just trying to find their way home but who got caught instead on the northern loop, bringing them right back to this same spot. Just once, they likely said to themselves, it would be helpful if the church took a stand on something and actually pointed the way.

William Trelawny found his way back to St. Jude's easily enough, though it had been maybe thirty-five years since he'd left. He had grown up here, an only child to parents who lived in a rented house out on the Twelfth Line. William — and it was always William, never Willy or Bill — was skinny and shy and never hung around with the other kids his age. The family made no effort to fit in, keeping to themselves. So William didn't play hockey and they didn't go to church.

But William had a gift, an achingly beautiful soprano voice. It was Miss Harkness, his fourth grade teacher, who coaxed it out of him and then got him to join the choir at St. Jude's, where she herself sang. Thereafter every Christmas Eve, in the glow of the candlelight procession, his clear solo voice would lead off the midnight service with the first verse of "Once in Royal David's City."

This soon became a Christmas tradition all its own. A deep hush would settle over the congregation as people closed their eyes and listened to that sweet unearthly sound, so close to them there in the darkness and yet so strangely distant, like the voice of an angel. Tears would appear on flushed cheeks and glisten like tiny stars in the flickering light. For some, it was precisely in those still moments, after all the baking and sewing and shopping, after all the long days and the shrinking dollar, that the Christ Child would come to them again.

Until his voice broke. No one heard much about William after that, and then the family moved away.

But people would still talk about the boy with the golden voice, usually at Christmas when some new child would be given the solo part, a part at which they were destined to fail. People would say, "It was really nice this year. But y'know, I can still hear that Trelawny kid clear as a bell. Now, *that* kid could sing!"

Trelawny had so entered the town's oral history that no one thought of him as having grown up. So when a tall man with a greying beard pulled up to the church in an old Volvo stationwagon just before the service one Sunday, people gave him the once-over side-glance they reserve for city folk and other suspicious strangers.

He walked with a slight stoop, suggesting a taller frame than he would have chosen for himself. His eyes were dark and his face was deeply lined, which made him a little frightening, except that his gaze seemed to be turned inward, like a man preoccupied. When he looked at you, it was with surprise, as if you had suddenly materialized out of nowhere in front of him. Or so Earl felt as he handed him a prayer book at the door.

The stranger took a seat in the back pew. Father David noticed him right away. When you have a congregation of thirty-five on a good Sunday, a visitor tends to stand out, especially a tall one, and there had not been many visitors lately. So Father David kept his eye on this newcomer, who sat by himself and didn't look up. At the offertory hymn, he stood with the rest, the hymn book open in his hand, but he did not join in the singing.

Following the service Father David was distracted as he shook hands at the door. He kept peering down the line of parishioners, waiting for the stranger to appear.

"Good morning, Father David." "Good morning, Keith."

"What cold hands you have this morning, Father." "Yes, Mrs. Bailey, but you know what they say…"

"Nice service, Father." "Thank you. Um, sorry, Harry, but did you mean 'sermon'?" "No, I meant 'service.' Good day now."

He shook the last hand and wandered back into the church. Did he go out by the sanctuary door, Father David wondered. Or down to the church hall? Father David made his way back up the aisle. Mrs. Goode, the organist, was packing up her music. "It seems you have a visitor," she whispered, looking meaningfully in the direction of the vestry. Father David saw the stranger's tall frame just inside the door.

"Hello," Father David called out. He approached the stranger and held out his hand. It was an awkward exchange, right in the doorway, so that the stranger had to back into the vestry to allow Father David to enter, bringing them into too close a proximity for two men who had just met. Father David squeezed past him, averting his eyes until he got round to the other side of the desk.

The stranger seemed to be preparing his thoughts. Father David waited for him.

"You don't know me," the man said, "but I used to come to this church. I used to sing in the choir."

"Really," Father David said. "That's great." Again he found himself waiting. "So," he ventured further, "where are you now?"

"I'm in the city. I'm at the university."

"Ah," said Father David and he began nodding his head, as if contemplating the depths of this new information. "So ... what brings you back now? Do you have family here?" he asked, still nodding.

"No," the stranger replied. "I want to be baptized."

Father David was taken aback. He might have considered he was on the brink of hearing some dark confession. He might even have expected a pitch for a handout. But baptism — this would not have crossed his mind.

Not that the notion of adult baptism was the least bit foreign to Father David. He had once written a masterful paper on the subject. Adult baptism, he had said, was to be the way of the future as whole generations of unbaptized adults would find their way back to church. He had argued that, in preparation for this eventuality, baptismal tanks should reappear in mainline churches and full immersion should once again become the norm for Christian baptism. It was a bold assertion, but he had put forward his case; he had stood his ground.

Now, however, he found himself shifting his weight slightly from one foot to the other. All he could think of to say was, "Isn't this a little out of your way?"

In the days that followed the word spread quickly that William Trelawny had returned. In fact, there was quite a buzz about town leading up to the baptism three weeks later, a day that had already been set aside for the baptism of the Trundle twins, Tara and Tiffany.

The church was half full and there was tangible excitement in the air, a sense of anticipation that had been missing that fall season. The twins were a handful, slipping around in their matching satin christening gowns. But it seemed to be their mother,

Daphne, who was the problem. Fussing continually, she passed them back and forth between their father and her sister, the godmother, whispering loud commands to each.

This was to have been her daughters' occasion, having personally booked it with "the Reverend" two months ago. She had been up late the night before, finishing the gowns, and had prepared a cold buffet that was waiting for family and guests at home. Meanwhile her husband, Tim, had chosen that morning to begin an oil change on the truck, until she hauled him in to wash up and get himself ready. He sat beside her awkwardly now, his tie askew, his blackened hands struggling to contain the squirming twosome.

They continued to squirm throughout their baptism, Daphne looking fierce as a candle was lit for each child. "Receive the light of Christ," Father David said as he handed the candles to the godmother, who couldn't find a place to put her prayer book, so tucked it in her armpit, "to show that you have passed from darkness to light."

After the Trundle twins had been "done," it was William Trelawny's turn. He moved slowly forward from the front pew and stood by the font. People craned their necks, trying to make out any resemblance between this dark weary man and the high angelic voice that rang so clearly in their memories.

He bent forward as Father David raised the baptismal shell to his head. "William John, I baptize you in the name of the Father … and of the Son … and of the Holy Spirit. Amen." The water poured down his forehead, collecting at the end of his nose. It ran onto his beard and dripped down onto his tie.

As Father David reached for the chrism, William raised his face. His eyes were closed, his brow arched in anticipation of the young priest's touch on his forehead. The morning sun shone down upon him through the baptistry window. Bathed in its warm glow, his face suddenly became that of a ten-year-old child, expectant and trusting. It was a truly remarkable transformation. Gone were the deep lines, gone was the dark gaze. It was in that instant that they recognized him.

At the end of the service, as Father David was reading the announcements, a strange thing happened, at least strange for St. Jude's. Father David was interrupted. He looked up. Wilf Smith was standing in his pew. "I was just saying, or wondering, if perhaps Mr. Trelawny here might like to honour us with a song, as many of us remember him from when he was a boy."

Father David did not know what to say. Mr. Trelawny looked down at his hands. A smile spread slowly across his face. Looking around from the front pew, he nodded his agreement. An excited murmur rippled through the congregation. Father David, trying not to appear put out, returned to his prayer desk and sat down.

Mr. Trelawny got up and spoke quietly to Mrs. Goode. "Why, of course I do," she beamed, digging into her bag and pulling out a dog-eared music book. He took his position at the top of the chancel steps, a little off to the side. Mrs. Goode began.

Suddenly, the church was filled with William Trelawny's rich baritone voice. He had chosen the Lord's Prayer, in a setting he had sung countless times as a boy. Mrs. Goode, focused intensely on the music before her, began swaying uncharacteristically on the organ bench. The congregation sat transfixed, barely breathing, until with the rising crescendo of the final cadence, William Trelawny came to the end. Only then, in the hush that followed, did some move a hand to wipe away a tear.

They never saw William Trelawny again. There was a reception in the church hall after the service, and people spoke with him. But then someone asked where he was, and he had gone — a middle-aged man on his way to somewhere, coming home to remember who he was.

Sweet Regret

I heard a confession today, an infrequent event in the life of an Anglican priest. The old adage that has governed our use of the rite, "All may; none must; some should," is understood by most Anglicans to mean we don't *do* confession. Which only means, of course, that "more should."

The problem seems to be vagueness. Every Sunday in churches across this country we join in confessing our sins, out loud and in public. Yet few think of it as real confession. It is more a kind of general sorriness for not being a better person, a mild affliction, which for its very fuzziness survives the absolution that follows and accompanies the penitent right up to the altar rail. There, kneeling with head bowed and hands raised, we grovel, still pretty much lost in our sin, to receive the "crumbs under thy table."

Somehow this is supposed to be satisfying. But as a result, believing we have paid our dues to sinfulness in general, Anglicans seldom experience the exhilaration of a specific sin, specifically forgiven.

And who could fault us? Confession is a painful business. It is not *meant* to be easy. It causes us to squirm and to sweat. It makes us face our feelings, something Anglicans are reluctant to do. Not that we don't *have* feelings. It's just that we would rather let them stew a bit until the opportunity arises to lend them some pageantry, like allowing them to leap out unannounced during the budget debate at the annual vestry meeting, or in unsigned letters to the rector evaluating recent changes in the Sunday liturgy.

So I was intrigued when Tom phoned me on Monday morning to make an appointment. He wanted me to hear his confession. Strange as it may sound, I felt a little excited by the prospect.

I don't know Tom well. Or didn't. He is a doer, not a talker, an active member of the property committee, the kind of guy who shows up at the church unexpectedly on a Saturday morning to change light-bulbs. Last spring, twelve years after he had agreed to fill in for a season, he finally retired from teaching the junior high Sunday school class. He'd been doing it so faithfully for so long that people almost forgot to thank him.

He would be approaching fifty now and balding a bit and is, as far as anyone could tell, a happy man. He is still married to Patsy, the lively woman he met at his first job at the municipal offices almost twenty-five years ago. They have two good kids.

Kevin is a computer whiz who last year in high school created a personal home page so sophisticated, with hypertext references and multi-media sound bytes and mini-action video sequences, that the board of education gave him a summer job to do the same for them.

Gaylene, his older sister, sports a black dyed crew cut these days, and a ring piercing her eyebrow. She prefers black T-shirts and black jeans and heavy steel-reinforced work boots. She wants to be an animation illustrator and, after a year wandering in Europe, is starting at art college in the fall. As I say, good normal kids.

So I admit my interest was piqued. I could tell by his voice, so low on the other end of the phone I wouldn't have recognized him, that this was not easy for him. We agreed to meet that day, on his way home from work. I prepared myself by setting aside my small stack of phone messages and trying to sit quietly until he arrived.

Maybe it's my own puritanical upbringing, maybe it's the damage done by the Victorian era, but when I think "confession," I think "sex." Somebody has done it with someone they shouldn't have, or they've thought about it. So, I figured, okay, Tom's had a fling. He's scared and he's confused and he wants the secret to lose its terrible power over him. He wants everything to go back to the way it was before.

I would not be able to give him that, of course. Forgiveness does not erase consequences. But I could promise him that God would be with him as he worked through whatever he had to do now. And I could promise myself not to take too great an interest in the details.

My own sexual awakening had come late, and had been even further delayed by a religious conversion the summer before I went off to university. I have to wonder now at the timing of that event, so convenient for someone scared to death of his own sexuality. That cold winter evening after class, when Maria pushed her body up against mine as we waited in the bus shelter, I had a ready excuse for my bashfulness — I was a born-again Christian.

I have often revisited that period of my life in my mind, slyly revising scenes like that one, pushing my conversion on a few years, like a death-bed penitent. "Paradise Lost" describes pretty well how those years seem to me now, looking back with a sigh.

In a way, such slow beginnings have suited me well for this my chosen profession. I read somewhere that 12 per cent of clergy are believed to have committed sexual indiscretions in the course of their pastoral work. I see this as a sad but real possibility, given their access to the personal lives of their parishioners and the accompanying power they can wield. But I tend to be the last one to know when such possibilities present themselves to *me*.

A while ago a young woman came to see me in my office. She was new to the parish and seeking advice on how she could get more "actively involved." She was tall and lithe, with the almond eyes and full lips of her Slavic ancestors. Her thick hair was pulled up and back, displaying long dangly earrings. She wore a short-sleeved turtle-neck sweater under a denim vest, and shorts so insubstantial they disappeared altogether as she casually crossed her thighs.

This exotic creature sitting opposite me, blushing slightly as she laid out her tenuous agenda, was the very vision of temptation itself. Yet all I wanted to do was drape my jacket around those slender shoulders and say, "There, there, dear. Wouldn't you be more comfortable with a little more on?" The last to know indeed.

Tom's countenance supported my suspicions. He arrived early and looked awful, his face an ashen grey, as if he had not slept in days. His tie was askew, his suit wrinkled. Sweat already dotted his brow.

We met in my office. I suggested we might talk it through first and then go into the church for the formal rite. He nodded his agreement without looking at me. We sat down. He leaned forward clasping his hands between his knees. I told him to take his time.

After several silent minutes I probed, "Tom? How do you want to begin?"

It all started at a funeral he had attended a few weeks ago. Someone in his office had died suddenly, a burst aneurism in his brain. He had been forty-three! Tom hadn't known him well, but still he shared the shock of it with his other middle-aged co-workers. It brought into focus the delicate thread that connects us with everything we know and hold dear.

He had arrived late; so he had to park a couple of blocks away from the funeral home, up a quiet residential street. It was in that old part of the city that has grown more gracious as the years have gone by, the trees lining the streets, tall and full, filtering the midday sun like a lush conservatory.

The service was hard. A brother-in-law tried to deliver a eulogy but broke down half-way through and had to sit down. Tom found it difficult to control his own emotions. He was grateful when it ended and the congregation poured out onto the lawn, finally to exhale. People lingered, not saying very much. When the time came to move on, he said a few good-byes and started back to his car.

The shade of the trees was cool and welcome. He loosened his tie and felt the breeze on the back of his neck. A short distance ahead he noticed two women in conversation on the sidewalk outside their homes. One had her back to him. She was elderly and gesturing broadly with both hands as she spoke, a purse looped over one arm. The other was young and stood listening, rocking a sleeping infant in a stroller.

He did not think much of this at first. He could not have told me anything distinguishing about either woman. It was just a pleasant diversionary scene as he walked to his car. But all this was about to change.

He glanced up to find the young woman looking at him. And he saw in an instant that she was not unattractive. She was short and blonde, her tanned skin shown off against the white-ness of a short-sleeved blouse and the crispness of khaki shorts. She was strikingly pretty, in a natural, almost athletic way, her boyish hair casually tossed back.

And then it happened.

Tom had to stop for a moment. He reached in his pocket for a handkerchief and held it to his eyes. He tried to choke back the little sobs bursting from his throat. I waited.

And then it happened. Their eyes met. It was like nothing that had ever happened to him before. It was not just that they looked at each other. It was more as if they looked *into* each other, as if they knew each other, and *had* known each other, perhaps always.

He was several steps away and his gait did not falter as he passed them. But their eyes stayed locked onto one another. Speechless, Tom felt lifted to some cosmic realm, some place outside of time, where perhaps they had once been lovers.

He paused again and let out an enormous sigh. It caught in his throat and became a moan. He put his hand over his mouth, stopping himself. He shook his head and said he was sorry. I encouraged him to go on.

He walked past her. When he reached his car he fumbled for his keys and found that he was shaking. It took both hands to get the key into the lock and open the door. He slid in and sat for a few minutes, both hands gripping the wheel.

What had just happened? Had he just imagined it, or had something powerful, something unearthly, just passed between him and a total stranger?

Finally he turned the key in the ignition. He pulled out and began making his way back down the street. As he approached the place they had met, he took his foot off the accelerator and allowed the car to slow. The older woman had gone, but the younger one stood on the walk where she had been before. As he rolled slowly by, uncertain whether to look or just to drive on, he glanced over. She was looking at him, her head cocked slightly to one side. As he looked on, she raised her hand about half-way, and waved.

So she knew, too. He wanted desperately to stop the car. He wanted to leap out and go to her. It was not clear what would happen next, but he didn't care. She possessed a part of him, and he knew in that instant he would never be the same again.

But he drove on. Slowly at first, but then picking up speed until he got to the corner. He looked back through the rear-view mirror, but she was gone.

He let out a sigh and for the first time raised his head to look at me. His eyes were filled with tears. He was finished.

I was caught off guard. That was it? I mean, it had been a touching story. And clearly it had had a profound effect on him. But he hadn't actually confessed anything, at least yet.

"Is there anything else, Tom?" I asked.

"No, that's it," he said. "Of course, I haven't been able to tell Patsy. I just couldn't, it would break her heart."

"But, Tom," I suggested, "nothing actually happened."

"That's not true!" he shot back, fixing me with a stare. "I loved another woman. I don't care if it was only for a passing instant. I loved her and she loved me just as surely as if we'd gone to bed together, as if I'd run off with her, never to return. That's how it feels."

His sense of guilt was real. He had experienced what felt to him like an infidelity of the heart, an alienation of his affections. But where was the sin? What he described was not lust, nor was it unfaithfulness. He had had powerful feelings of attraction, which apparently were shared. But there was no irretrievable action.

"There's nothing to forgive here, Tom," I said finally. "In fact, in a way, you're rather a lucky man. This is the stuff of poetry, the stuff young lovers die for. I guess the only question is, what will you do now?"

"What is there to do?" he said. "I think about going back to that street, of stopping in front of her house, of waiting for her to come out. But what would happen then? She would come out on the arm of some young guy and look up and see me, and I'd be sitting there like an idiot. Or maybe she'd come out alone and I'd say hello, and she would open her mouth to speak and have the voice of a truck driver." He permitted himself a slight dry chuckle. "I guess I don't want to know. I don't want that moment destroyed. I *want* for it to live on in my memory. But, God, it hurts."

We sat in silence for a few minutes. Then he stood, thanked me, shook my hand and left. I got my coat, locked up, and started for home, walking the kilometre or so to the house. I walked slowly, thinking about how strange love is.

Tom *was* lucky in a way. It happens all the time in movies, two people struck dumb as if by lightning, their paths scorched and their lives blown to hell. But that's not the way it usually happens in real life. For most of us, love is born of attraction certainly, but even more of commitment and hard work and years of knowing one another, of attending to one another.

As I put my hand on the door, I paused. What if things had turned out differently in my own life? What if I had met and married some woman other than my wife, and had made some other life for myself, with different children and a different home? What if then, already happily settled, I passed unknowingly my wife on the street? Would our eyes meet? Would we be aware of a parallel possibility, some other life that might have been? Would we recognize each other, even as strangers? Would we glance once, turn away and then look back, catching something of one another's soul in our gaze? Would we feel a sudden pang of regret?

I turned the knob. That would be the least we could do.

Chicken Soup

I was sitting down to lunch the other day when the telephone rang and out of the blue there was Father David at the other end.

We are not close. We greet each other as if we share an inside track, but we know each other hardly at all. Whatever bond we have derives from his serving the parish I used to serve, the rural parish of St. Jude's. He suspects I hear about him from my former parishioners (which, of course, I do), and I suspect he hears from them about me (which, more than likely, he doesn't!). Neither of us really wants to know for sure, fearing the worst.

When I asked him how things were going, he told me the annual Hog Fest was coming up. There was all the usual excitement, including the not-so-subtle jockeying for position among the Merry Widows who organize the event — from which, this year, Mavis McAteer seems to have emerged on top. This means that the women will likely have Alf Brown play his accordion up in the church while guests wait to be ushered to a free table down in the hall. We permitted ourselves a conspiratorial chuckle over these familiar politics. But this was not the reason for his call.

He was calling to get my advice. Had I, while I was at St. Jude's, ever taken a funeral for farm animals? Well, not a funeral exactly, more a memorial service. But the bodies would be present.

It took me a moment to get oriented to his question. If it were anyone else, I would have suspected a joke was coming. But Father David is an earnest young man. To whatever extent he has a sense of humour, he seems to regard it as little more than an obligatory social grace. The practical joke, the belly laugh — these would be quite unimaginable coming from Father David.

I told him I wasn't exactly sure what he meant.

He meant chickens. Had I ever been called upon to do some kind of funeral for chickens?

No, that had not been part of my experience at St. Jude's, I offered. Perhaps there were places where they did that kind of thing, but I really wouldn't know about it. Was someone asking for this?

It turned out someone was.

Marilyn DeCarre — she pronounces it Mary Lynn — is not a member of St. Jude's. She and her husband, Sterling, moved up to the area a few years ago, buying and renovating the old schoolhouse out at the Fifth Sideroad and Eleventh Concession. The schoolhouse was in use up until my time there, when a change in the school bus route removed the necessity of a school out in the middle of nowhere.

By the time the "For Sale" sign appeared, I guess it was looking pretty run-down. Tall grass had grown up around the foundation and bats had moved back into the belfry. It must have taken real imagination to see in that dilapidated old place a possible country home. But imagination is what Marilyn has plenty of.

Sterling is a corporate executive, a senior vice-president of a large marketing firm in the city. He has been taking a gradual retirement from the pressures of the business world and has managed to negotiate a new position with the firm as a kind of mentor for the up-and-coming junior executives.

It was a smart move. Those sassy young men and women had more energy than he did, and their ideas, culled from graduate business degrees and countless motivational seminars, wearied him with their smart-assed novelty. So he placed himself directly in their path, a few steps above them on the corporate ladder.

Marilyn is ten years Sterling's junior, and not your usual picture of a corporate wife. She used to be a kindergarten teacher and more recently taught art at a community college. She has been letting her long dark hair go grey naturally, and it cascades, thick and unruly, down to her shoulders. In she would bounce, unannounced, to Sterling's office in her long skirt, billowy blouse, and sandals, presenting without ceremony a bunch of spring flowers to Angela, her husband's pretty receptionist.

Marilyn has what some would call a sunny disposition. There are two hills for every valley, she never tires of saying. She has on many occasions surprised their friends with acts of unaffected munificence. At one dinner party she presented every guest with a personalized wooden salad bowl made by her art students, a memento of their "fellowship" together. Sterling laughed louder than was necessary as he hugged her shoulders, calling her his "hippy" bride.

She and Sterling have no children of their own. This was at Sterling's insistence. He is the father of two grown sons from a previous marriage and had no intention of repeating that role when he married Marilyn.

His retirement scheme included selling their large home in the suburbs and replacing it with both a "farm" in the country and a condo in the city. They were to live up at the farm, which he tended to refer to as "hers." The condo would be for when he had early meetings at the office or for when they wanted to spend a weekend in the city. However, it has turned out that he is working about as much as ever, staying overnight at the condo most nights now. Marilyn, left increasingly on her own up at the old schoolhouse, has thrown herself into creating her dream home.

Chickens were not originally part of the plan. In fact, apart from her cat, Marmalade (which she pronounces "Marmalad," the French way), Marilyn had not considered having animals on her farm at all. She envisaged something more akin to a thatch-roofed cottage set in the midst of an overgrown English country garden: an array of wild flowers as you approached the house from the drive — bright hollyhocks, purple fireweed, white lupin — and then fragrant climbing roses clinging to a trellised porch as you stepped up to the front door. She would cultivate roots and herbs and hang them to dry in her country kitchen.

But when she saw the ten dozen chicks down at Matty & Fern's Food and Hardware, she was smitten. Tufts of yellow fluff scurrying around under the heat lamp, peeping as they bumped into one another. They were like little balls of living sunshine, she thought, and bought the whole lot of them.

The schoolhouse had a lean-to at the back that had served as a small tool shed. Were Sterling so inclined, it would have been a great place to hang some power tools, oil a chain-saw, or give a tune-up to a riding mower. But he had been giving away his tools over the years. He took no satisfaction in physical labour, preferring to exercise his option of hiring those who did.

So the unpainted shed, with its padlocked door and small shuddered window, made a perfect chicken coop. Marilyn hung a lamp low over the middle of the dirt floor and nailed a few boards across the threshold, so the chicks couldn't run out into the yard.

Then every day she would throw wide the door, step over the barricade, and stand in the midst of her cheeping brood as they ran to greet her, their sun-ringed Goddess of Plenty, casting feed like a sower, giving life to her little family. Maybe it was the maternal instinct, maybe the sweet smell of the country air, but on some days the sheer joy of it almost brought tears to her eyes.

Marilyn had not asked anything about the chicks when she bought them. Matty had given her some instructions for the early weeks about keeping them warm and fed. He did say, though, that they were a fast-growing breed, intended for a quick trip at minimal expense to the poultry operations that supplied the fast-food chains. All she saw were little fluffy orphans in search of a mom.

But by the time the chicks were big enough to be let out into the outdoor pen, they were beginning to make Marilyn nervous. Their rush to her feet was becoming more like a swarm, and she could feel the pecking of little beaks through the toes of her rubber boots. They were not as cuddly as they grew into their rushed pre-adolescence, and some seemed actually to be growing up deformed.

This was confirmed the day she found the first victim of mob violence, a stunted chick with only one leg. How had she missed this, she wondered. The poor thing never stood a chance in the daily feeding frenzy. Its miserable disfigurement must have aroused blood-lust in the others.

She noticed there were other misfits growing up unnaturally, without a wing or a leg, hobbling around the fringes of the pack. Soon there were more victims. She picked up their lifeless little bodies and placed them in separate plastic freezer bags, zip-locking the tops. She laid them in a shoe box, side by side, and buried them out in the pasture.

It made her look at her flock differently, suspiciously. There were murderers in this bunch. The light pecking at her toes at feed time became a horrible sensation. Would they peck at her eyes if she were to stumble and fall into their midst? She began to listen for them as she lay in her bed at night. Would they wonder where the feed was kept? Would they dig with their little feet an escape tunnel under the chicken wire? Would they come scratching at the door?

All the while they continued to grow at an alarming rate, leaving behind the carcasses of those who couldn't keep up, their bodies bloodied, their eyes gouged out. She tried to get hold of Sterling at his office, but the temporary receptionist — an unfamiliar voice — told her he was "unavailable."

Finally she had had enough. This was not fun anymore. In fact, it had become creepy and far removed from the English country garden of her dreams. So she called Matty.

No, he couldn't take them back, he said. But if she could wait a few more weeks, they'd be almost ready for slaughter anyway, and then she could call Kate Morton, the butcher, to come and do the deed.

Marilyn was not sure she could wait. When she called Kate, she was told it would be a shame to slaughter them so early. But Kate herself would try to find someone who could take the chickens off her hands until they were marketable. That night there was no answer at the condo, so Marilyn left a message asking Sterling please to call her as soon as possible.

Marilyn waited two days and then called Kate Morton again. No, she hadn't found anybody to take a hundred chickens, not even for free. But the birds could be slaughtered early, if that was what Marilyn wanted. They wouldn't have a lot of meat on them, but she could freeze them for stews, and they'd make good soup, of course.

So last Thursday, Kate came over in her Mazda pick-up, "Morton's Poultry Service" painted merrily on the side, with the head of a happy chicken up in the corner near the cab. Kate was not a large woman, but she walked with the square gait of a man. In her hooded sweatshirt and black rubber apron and gloves, swinging a hatchet in her hand, she looked more like a crazed killer from a B-grade movie than a businesswoman.

Marilyn said from the door she was not sure she could watch. Kate said the price would be considerably lower if she could help out a bit. But it was not the price that persuaded Marilyn to participate in the slaughter. As they walked together over to the run, and she looked down upon the doomed flock, the full burden of her decision fell heavily upon her. She had nurtured these little creatures into the world, even the murderous ones who, after all, were only acting from instinct, not out of any evil intent. She should see it through to the end.

So Kate got to work. She had a swift and efficient method, the result of years of experience in her line of work. She first smacked a bird on the side of its head with the broad side of the hatchet, stunning it. Then she grabbed it by the throat, scooped it up and swung it around once in the air until the neck cracked. The bird landed hard on the chopper block and, WHACK, off came its head. The operation took all of five seconds.

Marilyn's job was to tie the feet with wire and carry the bleeding carcasses to the shed, where they were to be hung from the rafters and drained. This would make the plucking easier when Kate came back with a work crew in the afternoon.

The killing went on through most of the morning. Kate kept up a running commentary on anything that came into her head:

the unseasonable weather, the kind of people she didn't like, the spectacular spill at last evening's monster truck rally. But Marilyn wasn't listening and, in any case, could not have responded. A dry lump had lodged itself in her throat. Tears blurred her vision as she picked up the twitching carcasses. Every time the hatchet came down she thought she was going to be sick.

By the end of the morning, a hundred chickens were hanging lifeless in the shed, their blood collecting in pools on the earthen floor and running in small rivulets into the shadows. Kate went for lunch and Marilyn was left alone with the bodies, beside herself with horror and grief. All her hopes, all her best intentions, and this was the result! It felt like a sign. From a deep inner place too dark for words an aching realization began to surface. That was when she called Father David.

She was not a church-goer, so she didn't know who she was calling exactly. Nor did she know what to ask. But his voice sounded like solace to her, and she broke down and sobbed into the phone. He reassured her it was all right, she should just take her time.

Technically there is no funeral service for chickens. But I think Father David will have his pastoral work cut out for him, anyway. And then maybe there'll be someone new to help out with the Hog Fest. The Merry Widows have been complaining that it's always the same ones who do the work. For years they've done it all — buttered the buns, diced the cabbages, sliced the ham, simmered the soup. It's time some of the young ones pitched in. They'd be more than willing to show her how it's done.

Brotherly Love

Be careful what you pray for, the saying goes, because you just might get it! Like "brotherly love," for example. It's something we in the church commonly pray for, one way or another. But are we really ready for it? And would the world thank us for such a gift?

This is one instance where I really am talking about brothers, with apologies to the inclusive language watchdogs, the "Kin for Inclusive Liturgical Language," or "KILL," as they are commonly known. Maybe it's the same with sisters, but I wouldn't know about that.

What I do know is that brotherly love consists of both a mutual love and a mutual hatred, co-existing in the same instant. My brother and I love each other. My brother and I hate each other. This is not a contradiction. But when we are in close proximity to one another, the result can be frequent and rather violent explosions.

Growing up, I hated my brother for his merciless taunting, his twilight mind control through our early years when we shared a bedroom. He was going to a rodeo, he would tell me, riding into town on a splendid white stallion. But unless I did everything he told me to, unless I became his slave, I would have to ride behind him — on a turtle. "No, not a turtle!" I would beg him. "Yes, a turtle!" he would say.

But years later when, as solo trumpeter, he flubbed the "Last Post" in front of the entire school at the Remembrance Day service, missing notes, losing his place, my embarrassment was for his sake, not my own. And the day at the kitchen sink when I wound up and socked him in the solar plexus, winding him, his lungs sucking for air in whistling gasps, I ran away to my bedroom and hid, shaking with shame.

Brotherly love is not gentle. Things get broken, usually things belonging to other people. Parents come running, crowds gather, police are called in. Meanwhile the two brothers help each other up, slap one another on the back, and walk off together to shoot a few hoops.

I was reminded of this recently after I had preached a sermon on the theme of filial love. I said that realizing we are all related helps us to see one another in a new light. It helps us be a bit more understanding, a bit more tolerant. That was the day the McBrides, with a wry smile, approached me at the coffee hour to relate a recent story of filial love from their own household.

Stan and Judy McBride would be in their late forties. Steven and Darryl are their oldest children, fraternal twins. The boys are both tall and good looking, both natural athletes, both bright; but any similarity ends there.

Steve is the oldest by about three minutes. He is solid like his dad and played any high school sport that allowed him to tackle somebody or otherwise rough them up. This meant football, of course, but he preferred rugby because the contact was uninhibited by all those pads and almost unrestricted by rules. During the winter season he fought on the wrestling team, helping take the school to the provincial finals a few years ago.

But for all that, he is not an aggressive person. He's just physical. At school he used to sneak up behind the younger kids, the seventh and eighth graders, and pick them up clear off the floor in a rough and tumble bear hug, growling and snorting like a wild animal. It would scare the hell out of them, and they would yelp and shriek as their books and lunches were sent scattering down the hall. But no one ever reported it. That was because they liked him doing it. He was the only older kid in the school who paid them even the slightest attention, and his sudden attacks were taken as a kind of initiation rite into adolescence.

Darryl, on the other hand, is lean like his mom and was all elbows and knees growing up. He is quick and smart and became the school's first true basketball star, his picture taking centre place amid the trophies and pennants in the display case outside the office. He is quieter than his brother, but equally self-possessed. Whereas Steve lives life passionately on its surface, possessing no more and no less than what you see, Darryl lurks in life's depths, waiting for his move. When you get hit by Darryl, whether on the basketball court or in debate, you get stung, because you don't see it coming.

Darryl is also diabetic, a crushing discovery for a fifteen-year-old, back when he was diagnosed. He has learned to live with it, though he has had some close calls as youthful recklessness tempted him off the wagon of his strict diet and regular injections. His parents still don't know about the weekend at the cottage when Steve and some of their friends sped across the lake at two in the morning to get Darryl to the emergency clinic in town as he slipped deeper into an alcohol-induced coma. Every one of them grew up a little that night.

Steve and Darryl have always been close. Their "elephant antics," as their mother called them — running full force down the stairs, rough-housing in the tiny bedroom they shared — caused the floors of the house to shake and the windows to rattle in their frames. Their dad half expected that one day, when he and Judy were ready to sell the house and retire on its appreciated value, it would be found to have shifted so precariously on its foundation that it would have to be demolished instead.

When choosing career paths, the boys went off in different directions, Steve toward engineering, Darryl to business administration. But it is not surprising that they still managed to choose the same university, getting adjacent rooms in the same residence.

The residence, known colloquially as Beaver House, was constructed of grey concrete blocks so typical of colleges and universities built in the sixties and seventies. These were as much compounds as schools, designed with youthful rebellion in mind by planners who had no intention of seeing *their* buildings shift on their foundations. But as a cost-cutting concession, every pair of rooms was separated not by concrete, but by a double plaster wall.

Each room was a mirror image of the one on the other side: a low bed against the far wall, a compact closet at its foot, a desk facing the inside wall with bookshelves mounted above. The decor was Spartan, to be sure, but it felt like luxury to most undergraduates, who plastered the walls and ceilings with posters, and tossed their unwashed clothes about for added texture. This meant the small windows looking out onto the quad became essential for ventilation, especially between visits to the laundromat, and were propped open by empty beer bottles right through the coldest winter days, causing forced-air furnaces in some distant physical plant to work non-stop night and day.

Both Steve and Darryl are good students, working at their desks late into the night if need be. But their study habits are unrecognizable, one from another. Darryl keeps the desktop clear and uncluttered, constantly reorganizing his books and notes as he goes. His laptop computer sits open and ready nearby, as does a fountain-pen, given him by his grandfather, which he uses for calligraphy whenever a creative urge strikes him.

Steve's style is somewhat more chaotic. He is in constant motion, most of the time searching for something he has just put down, perhaps a useable quote he was sure was just a few pages back, perhaps a CD to load in the portable boom box he keeps by his elbow on the desk. Whatever study materials he needs are salvaged from a stash of personal effects stuffed into his desk drawer, including key-chains, pop cans, car magazines, and gum wrappers.

During late-night sessions, as a stress-reducing habit, it was not uncommon for Steve to break into a drum solo, using a couple of pencils for drumsticks, his desk surface as a snare, textbooks and notes as cymbals, and various sonorous portions of the wall as tom-toms. Darryl, on the other side, would hear this, signalling it was time for a break. Waiting for an entry, Darryl would answer with a rhythm on his side of the wall. Steve would pick it up, and for a few frenzied minutes the two would go at it in rock 'n' roll ecstasy until one or the other would shove his chair away from the desk, get up, and go down the hall for a pop or for a bathroom break.

One winter night, as Steve and Darryl were preparing for mid-terms and cabin fever was running high throughout the residence, Darryl heard the familiar sounds of Steve's release valve.

Tic-ticka-tacka-tacka. Tic-ticka-tic-tic. Darryl looked at the wall and realized he had not been studying anyway. He had been staring into space, without a single recognizable thought to show for it. He listened to the tom-toms beating from amid the desktop jungle next door. He felt tired, too tired to respond. But then he got an idea.

The year before, Darryl had worked at a summer camp for diabetics. Sometimes late at night the staff had amused themselves by waging water wars with long-needled hypodermics stolen from the infirmary. A battle would start when someone would puncture the soft paperboard walls that separated the rooms of the staff lodge and empty the contents of the needle into the room next door. Off the staff would go from there, spilling out of their rooms into the hallway and eventually down to the waterfront for the grand finale. At the end of the summer Darryl had tucked a few syringes in with his stuff, thinking these might come in handy some day. He realized now that that day had arrived.

As Steve beat on the snare of his desk drum kit, Darryl dug out a syringe. He filled its large chamber with diet Coke and, taking a moment to judge the angle, plunged the needle through the wall. The drumming continued. Holding the needle steady, Darryl shot its contents forward, and waited. The drumming stopped.

Darryl withdrew the syringe and prepared a second hit. Again he lined up the needle and let the contents go. "Shit," he heard from the other side. "Shit! What the ...?" Then Steve's tone changed. This is what Darryl was waiting for. "Oh, no," Steve was saying. "Oh, no, you don't, you bastard. No, you don't. This means war!"

Darryl prepared to reload. But something was making its way through the wall. It was withdrawn. As Darryl bent to take a closer look, a pencil shot back through like a missile, catching him in the eye, a direct hit. He reeled backward, falling over the chair. He pressed the palm of his hand to his injured eye. It was watering badly, but he would live.

Darryl could hear Steve muttering through the wall. He groped for his fountain-pen. It was loaded. Barely taking time to aim, he shoved it in the hole and released the whole cartridge. "Sh-sh-shit!" came the reply. He could hear papers being scooped up. He could hear Steve's desk being cleared, books being salvaged, things thrown to the floor. Damage had been done.

Darryl went quickly to the door and locked it. When he returned, standing well back from the wall, it suddenly occurred to him that the laptop lay dangerously close to the path of return fire. He hunched down, approached, and grabbed it off the desk. He could hear what sounded like furniture being moved in Steve's room. He waited.

For a moment all was quiet. Then, in a scene he would later replay in slow-motion in his head, still disbelieving, a fist came crashing through the wall. Instinctively Darryl leapt backward onto the bed. The hand, failing to connect with its intended victim, began groping madly around for something, anything it could grab and destroy, papers, books, anything. "I'll get you, you shit-brain!" Steve was yelling. The hand was retracted.

Darryl, standing on the bed, was caught between exhilaration and alarm. Maybe things were getting a little out of hand. But Steve was not through. Darryl waited. He heard Steve grunt. The wall exploded. Plate-sized chunks of plaster hurtled through the room as the legs of a desk chair burst through the wall. The bookshelves leapt from their brackets above Darryl's desk, collapsing in a heap, books scattering across the floor.

As the dust settled, Darryl was startled to be able to see Steve on the other side, standing with his feet apart, wearing his sweat pants and T-shirt, ink stains on his hands, the chair lodged between them. Voices could be heard out in the hall.

"Holy shit," Darryl offered quietly as he got down off the bed and approached the hole in the wall. Three of the chair's legs had made it through, one completely, the others just with their tips. Steve couldn't suppress a look of pride. "Pretty good, eh?" he said.

When the chair was dislodged it left a gaping hole over two feet in length and almost as wide. The brothers looked at each other through the wall. There would be no easy way to repair the damage. The only immediate answer was camouflage.

So for the rest of the term Steve's poster of Miss Corvette 1959 pouted down at him when he sat pouring over books and tapping out rhythms with his pencils. Likewise, Darryl's Navajo rug found a new home, its bright colours dancing before his eyes as he tried to read late into the night.

Amazingly, the incident was soon forgotten, even as the two now spoke freely with one another through their respective wall coverings. Occasionally they would hand a calculator back and forth, brushing aside Miss Corvette's curvaceous hips. Or one's face would suddenly appear, saying, "Hey, you want to go for a beer?" Any sense of guilt was overridden by their satisfaction with this new arrangement. Until the term ended, and they had to move out.

They studied the problem. They could try to plaster the wall themselves. But it was year-end and neither had the fortitude — or the money, for that matter — to stick around and see the job properly done. They could just leave the wall coverings up. But what would be the point? The hole would be discovered *and* they would lose their stuff. There was no reasonable alternative. They did what anyone would do who had made a mess of things and was then overwhelmed by the consequences. They walked away.

It was mid-June when Stan and Judy opened the mail to find a bill from the university, a repair bill for $522.66. By that time, Steven and Darryl had long since finished the semester and were both conveniently away on far-flung summer jobs. Steve was planting trees somewhere in central British Columbia; Darryl was a junior bookkeeper at a mine in northern Ontario. So their parents had to wait a week or so to get the whole story from their boys. And then, of course, they got two stories.

Well, Steve and Darryl will be paying for the repairs. And writing a letter of apology to the university. And covering next year's residency costs themselves. This was, after all, not the sort of thing that made parents proud. Their kids were not raised to be so reckless. It was an irresponsible act, silly and dangerous. Someone could have been hurt.

The boys received their sentences, handed down in separate phone calls, with solemn attentiveness, especially the part about paying their own way next year. That would surely mean that they would need part-time jobs to keep them in books and beer money, and that Steve's hopes of buying a car with his summer's earnings were dashed. These were serious consequences indeed for one stupid act.

But telling me about it over coffee after church, their dad had to admit that it was also kind of funny, though Judy looked askance at him as he said this. He had barely been able to maintain his stern parental voice on the phone, he said. Which was strange, because he *had* been outraged by their stupidity. But as the facts came to light, he realized how much he loved his sons, and how much they loved each another, albeit in a primitive, male sort of way.

So it just makes me think. Brotherly love? A nice concept. But who would pick up the pieces?

A Prayer Stool
for Paul

Father David has a prayer stool in his study. You have to admire a priest who has a prayer stool in his study. These days you have to admire a priest who prays, period.

It blows the popular perception, I know, but apart from Sundays and holidays most priests don't pray. They get up in the morning, shower, grab a cup of coffee, and then go to the office, just like most of their parishioners. The only difference is that sometimes the office is downstairs rather than downtown.

A normal workday might include promising to pray for a troubled parishioner, or putting the finishing touches on the upcoming ecumenical Prayers for Peace service at the cenotaph, or even leading the evening prayer and meditation group. But it is the exception rather than the rule that priests start their day on their knees, petitioning the good graces of a Supreme Being without whom, after all, they wouldn't have a job.

Father David has a prayer stool in his study, though, and he actually uses it — for prayer! This has been his daily practice since his divinity school days. Even as a young man, he was someone who liked routine; so, living in residence, every morning began the same way. He would swish down to the dining hall for breakfast in his academic gown, take a coffee to the graduate student lounge for a selective read of the *Globe and Mail,* and then make his way to the chapel, arriving at precisely 8:25.

This was the time the student officiant-for-a-day usually would rush in to the sacristy, glance at the instructions left by the chaplain, rummage through the closet for an alb their size, throw it over their head, emerge a few moments later to light the candles, then kneel at the prayer desk only to discover they had left their prayer book back in the sacristy. Eventually they would settle down to lead the dozen or so students and faculty who had gathered for Morning Prayer.

David, by virtue of his consistency, sitting in the same place day after day — aisle seat, third pew, epistle side — and because he himself was a stickler for liturgical detail, proved a godsend to the first-year students. They were each expected to officiate at the morning service and were graded on their performance by the dean, a small dark man in a black academic gown who sat at the back, actually taking notes. But few had the panache to carry it off.

So each day David would end up leaning forward to answer their whispered last-minute questions: "You light the epistle candle first, then the gospel candle," he would whisper back. "The gospel candle is the one on the left." Mid-service, when a neo-phyte officiant became confused and lost his way, David would give a discreet nod, telepathically directing him to, "Sit down now."

This was a role for which David had never applied, to which he had never been appointed, and for which he never received any official thanks. His reward, as they say, is great in heaven, meaning simply that now, almost ten years later, he is still saying the daily office every morning while most of his classmates break out in a cold sweat just thinking about it.

Of course, Father David has the advantage of coming from a family of clergy. His father was a parish priest, his grandfather a bishop. Every morning of his life he saw his father dip a piece of dry toast into a cup of black coffee while standing at the kitchen door, then kiss his mother and make his way across the yard to the church for Morning Prayer. Most mornings, the young David knew, his father prayed alone, though it was announced in the bulletin and on the roadside sign:

𝔐orning 𝔓rayer
Weekdays at 8:30 a.m.
Saturdays at 9 a.m.
𝔄ll 𝔚elcome

The Saturday adjustment was a concession to people's work lives and to their apparent need to grab a few extra minutes of sleep on the weekends. But the gesture was in vain. Even the altar guild, arriving Saturday mornings to prepare the church for Sunday, would assemble in the kitchen, waiting for David's father to finish "saying his prayers" before getting down to their work.

The prayer stool was David's own innovation. He bumped into one during a divinity class retreat at the Order of the Incarnation, an Anglican monastery in upstate New York. For formal prayer the monks sat collegiate style, facing one another across a stone chancel. The guests sat in the nave, facing forward.

But in the apse, tucked away out of sight behind the high altar, was a tiny chapel, just right for private prayer. Apart from a miniature sanctuary containing an altar, a credence table, and a prayer desk, the little chapel was unfurnished. Midway through the morning a small stained glass window high above the altar permitted one single beam of light to form a spot in the middle of the chapel floor. Here Brother Nhat, a former Vietnamese Buddhist monk, practised his daily meditation on a low wooden prayer stool.

David came upon him suddenly and quite by accident while looking for the sacristy. He had been told that if he wanted to see how a sacristy ought to be designed, he should see the one at Incarnation. So in search of the sacristy he rounded the corner at the end of the long corridor outside the chancel and almost fell over Brother Nhat, who was kneeling motionless in the middle of the chapel floor.

It impressed David that Brother Nhat showed not the slightest awareness of his presence, even as he teetered precariously above him, trying to regain his balance. The little monk was clearly beyond earthly disturbance. David stole a hasty retreat but not before noticing the elegant yet simple stool on which the tranquil monk rested.

It consisted of three slim boards, one comprising the seat, the other two the supports. The seat, angled slightly forward, supported the weight of the monk while allowing him to tuck his feet beneath the seat in a low kneeling posture. It was a natural hybrid of the traditional pew kneeler, which inevitably strains your back and hurts your knees, and the lotus position, which places you on a cold draughty floor, causing your arthritic joints to flare up. It accommodated in a wonderful economy both physical relief and inner attentiveness, the twin needs of the true man of prayer.

Later that day, David saw Brother Nhat out in the vegetable garden, turning over the long rows that had recently produced carrots and turnips, the sleeves of his habit rolled up to his elbows. David called out to him and approached in a friendly manner. The monk straightened up, shielding his eyes from the sun.

"Hi," David said. "I came across you this morning in the Lady Chapel. I hope I didn't disturb you." The little monk smiled. It was difficult to determine his age. His body was taut like a young man's and his face was open and round. But the lines were deep at the corners of his eyes and David noticed the tell-tale brown spots of age on the backs of his hands.

"I was wondering about that prayer stool you use," David continued. "It looked really useful."

The monk's expression grew serious. He thought for a moment. "What you ask not easy thing. I will see." He nodded and smiled and went back to his work.

David stood there for a moment, wondering what had just transpired between them. The monk looked up at him. "I will see," he said again, nodding. David thanked him, and gave a slight bow, though this was certainly not his custom, and then walked away, trying to look nonchalant.

Two days later the retreat was ending and David and the others were assembling their bags in the large vestibule. Everyone's spirits were high and Brother Raymond, the guest master, was being his jovial self, asking if there were any takers for the religious life. The life was hard, he said, but the pay was no good. Everyone laughed.

Suddenly Brother Nhat appeared, looking a little flustered. He surveyed the small crowd for a moment. When he saw David, he looked at him quizzically, as if uncertain. "For you," the monk said, and he handed David a prayer stool. He gave him a low bow and turned to walk away.

"Thank you," David said, startled. "Thank you very much!" The small monk looked over his shoulder, smiling, a sparkle in his eyes. He nodded again and then disappeared.

The stool was new, with the outdoor smell of freshly cut pine. It consisted of three slim boards arranged as a seat with two supports. The supports were attached to the underside of the seat not by screws but by glue and by dowelling, which had been inserted through the seat and then sanded smooth. The dimensions of the stool achieved a perfect harmony between form and function. David rode home with the prayer stool on his lap, running his fingers over the clean joints and the sanded surfaces.

Father David was more proud of this possession than just about anything else he owned. Once at a clergy conference, in a workshop entitled "Faith Priorities for Personal and Professional Fulfilment," he was asked, if his house were on fire and he could retrieve only one possession, what would it be? He thought first of the piano, but that was dumb. He thought of his and Beverley's photo albums, but then it hit him — the stool! That is what he would go back into a burning house to get.

Every morning Father David kneels at his prayer stool and says the daily office. There, among the psalms and the readings, the collects and canticles, his soft voice rises and mingles with the crashing cacophony of Beverley in the kitchen next door. She is the very model of domestic industry, slapping bologna on bread for lunches, turning the bacon as it sizzles in the pan, giving the toaster lever that firm double click that makes it take hold, all in the inimitable way she does everything — with zest, with the clashing of dishes and the slamming of cupboard doors, with the radio announcer droning away unheeded, and Beverley herself humming a merry tune.

None of this is a distraction to Father David, though. He long ago accepted it in the one big love with which he has allowed Beverley to enfold his life into hers. If the truth were known, he is probably happiest in this their morning ritual, this daily offering of their very different selves to God.

Miraculously, neither Paul nor Catherine, their two children, are awakened by the morning sounds of their mother in the kitchen. They take it all in during those final moments of sleep, as from some floating billowy cloud, a drawer of cutlery descends, scattering in slow motion across the tiled floor. They raise their sleepy heads from their pillows, recognize as from a distant land the familiar sounds of morning, and then drift back to sleep.

One morning last week, though, Paul, who is five, appeared in the doorway of his father's study, his blanky in tow. He stood sleepily for a moment, watching his dad kneeling at the prayer stool. "What are you doing, Dad?" he asked.

David looked round. "Hi, bud. What are you doing up?" Paul rubbed his eyes and yawned. "I'm saying my prayers," David told him. "Do you want to join me?"

"No," Paul answered. "What do you do?" he asked, walking over.

David got himself up off his knees and sat down at his desk chair. He held out his hands. Paul shuffled over and leaned into his dad's chest. "Well, I read the Bible," David said, "I talk to Jesus, and then I write a little in my journal."

Paul thought about this for a few moments. "I have a journal, too," he said. "I let people look at it if they want. I draw in it mostly." Paul gently pushed himself off his dad and walked unsteadily toward the door. There he paused and turned back. "Could I have a stool like yours?" David smiled. "We'll see," he said.

That day, after lunch, Father David visited the lumber store. Making his way slowly along the racks of pre-cut lumber, he picked up board after board, turning each one over in his hands, until he came to a piece of unblemished pine. He got some wood glue, a new bit for his drill, and some quarter-inch dowelling. That evening after supper he went out to the garage and began.

The seat would have to be longer than the supports, though not too long. The supports had to be cut in such a way that the seat would be angled slightly forward. He considered using the router to help position the supports in grooves under the seat, but then thought better of it. He wrote out fractions on some scrap cardboard with his carpenter's pencil until he had each measurement exact. He cut the pieces with his power saw and positioned them for fit and size.

Yesterday, Paul again stumbled into the study to look in on his dad. There on the floor, beside where his dad was kneeling, was a prayer stool, a little smaller than his dad's. David looked round at his son and smiled at him.

Paul went out of the room, returning a few minutes later with his sketch-pad journal. As his dad resumed his prayers, Paul sat down next to him on the stool, his knees drawn up in front of him, and started to sketch. From the kitchen came the cheery sounds of Beverley singing.

Forgiveness

The kids have all been sent to their rooms. Little feet have stomped on floorboards, toys have been thrown about, doors slammed. My wife is now pacing the hallway, breathing fire, and reading the riot act through the walls. I am being smart. Having risen indignant in the midst of the fray to give everyone my sternest and fiercest look, I have now retreated to my study. I am staying out of the way.

If this is the usual scenario, we will have a breakthrough in about seven minutes. Somewhere a door will slowly open and a quiet teary voice will call out, "Sorry." My wife will kneel on the floor and hug each one — or perhaps all of them together — and begin negotiating the appropriate restitution. And that, hopefully, will be that. At least for now.

Forgiveness ought to be a way of life. It is not, of course. It is rather a way *back* to life when we have lost our way. And it is never easy, especially among kin. But the alternative is unthinkable. It is a form of death.

Daniel and Donny Lucas grew up on a sprawling dairy farm not far from St. Jude's, my first parish. The farm had been in the family for five generations. It was understood that one day it would go to Daniel, the oldest. So when the opportunity presented itself, old Mr. Lucas purchased the hundred acres that bordered him on the north. This would be for Donny, the younger of the two brothers, when he was ready for it. In the meantime it could be leased out.

The northern hundred was separated from the Lucas farm by a small woodlot. The boys grew up playing in that woodlot. In the summer, after chores were done, the long hot afternoon sun would drive them into the cool shade of the elms and birches. There they made forts from which they lobbed dried mud balls at unsuspecting cows that strayed their way. There, lying on their backs on the cool earth, sharing their daydreams about hockey and cars — and, eventually, about girls — they measured the slow movement of the sun across the sky and the slow turning of the seasons that led to manhood.

Donny worshipped his older brother and followed him everywhere. In the school yard he was Daniel's constant shadow, moving within Daniel's protective sphere beyond the reproach of teachers and the abuse of ballpark bullies. Daniel just had that way about him — a quiet, self-contained confidence and a wisdom beyond his years — earning him the instinctive respect of everyone around him.

Moving out of the old family farmhouse was not easy for Donny, though this was not something he knew how to talk about. When he married Eileen, a perky girl from a neighbouring county, they built a house and barn at the top end of his new property, just off the second concession. The house was a trim white bungalow, placed squarely in the middle of a treeless yard. Eileen planted flower gardens on three sides of the house and graced the windows with lace curtains, but years later the house still appeared new and, apart from the addition of an above-ground pool in the backyard, barely lived in.

By way of contrast, across the driveway stood the barn, which, after only a few years, looked like it had been there for generations. Its concrete foundation was splattered with red mud, the paint hung in long peeled strips off the auxiliary shed, bits of machinery littered the dirt compound. Donny had never been one for appearances.

He and Daniel cleared a rough road through the woodlot, allowing the brothers passage back and forth for the borrowing of farm equipment, and also for Donny to have a shortcut when he went into town. So at first it seemed to Donny that he'd hardly left home at all. In those early days, when Eileen was working in town, he would arrive for the noon-day meal as always, served up on heaping platters by Mrs. Lucas. The conversation among the men would be sparse, old Mr. Lucas presiding over its quiet ebb and flow beneath Mrs. Lucas's caustic commentary on all the fresh disasters in and around the community.

It never would have occurred to Donny to do otherwise, and why should it have? But after the birth of Sean, their first child, Eileen quit her job to be a full-time mom and farm wife, and she quickly grew resentful of the magnetic pull of Donny's family. So over time Donny's daily visits slowed to a trickle until eventually, to Eileen's satisfaction, they stopped altogether. He found himself drawn more and more from his own familiar surroundings into a new world, Eileen's world, a world of children and in-laws and acquaintances that were not his own.

Meanwhile, driving every day through the woodlot on his way into town or to borrow the back-hoe, Donny observed his brother's world growing and flourishing a hundred-fold, pressed down, running over. First their father bought the ninety-five acres across the road when the McClintocks had to sell. After his father's stroke, Daniel turned it into soy beans, one of the first in the county to do so and the first to actually turn a profit at it. A few years later he encouraged his father to apply for a research grant that permitted them to participate in nation-wide experiments with artificial insemination. The farm thrived and his reputation grew.

When Mr. Lucas died the whole operation fell squarely onto Daniel's shoulders, including the care of his mother, whom most people regarded as "difficult." Daniel was just about the only one who could reason with her, though he usually preferred simply to let her talk herself through the emotional spectrum from outrage to annoyance to silence to conciliation, and eventually to the point where she could laugh at the whole damn thing. As a consequence, he was the only one she would ever listen to, her oldest boy who had grown up so big and smart and filled with that quiet determination she had so loved in his father.

When Daniel met and married Margaret a few years later, as the custom was and still is in most farming communities, she moved into his home and came under the watchful eye of her new mother-in-law, in whose opinion Margaret was one of those modern girls who had never learned a thing right and who had to be taught everything all over again.

Margaret would work away in the kitchen with her mother-in-law sitting in the old pressed-back rocker, not saying much but saying too much for the likes of Margaret — things like, "Myself, I never would try to make pastry on a day so humid, but I guess that's the way things are being done today." "I guess so, Mom," Margaret would answer, and she would drop the rolling-pin down on the dough with a mighty whack.

Over time Mrs. Lucas's health began to fail, as she reminded her daughter-in-law almost daily, and eventually they moved her bedroom down to where the dining-room used to be, beside the kitchen. As she became more bedridden, Mrs. Lucas would be close at hand if she needed help with anything, which she did about every five minutes or so, it seemed to Margaret, who by this time had three pre-school children to contend with as well.

It was not long before this all proved too much for Margaret. Daniel pleaded quietly with his mother to back off a bit and give his wife some space, let her do things her own way, but to no avail. Finally Margaret confronted her husband. It would either be her or his mother, she said, but one of them would have to go, and she hoped he didn't really have to think about it. So it was resolved that they would move Mrs. Lucas into the nursing home in town, where she could receive the proper care and attention she needed. They didn't tell her or anyone else about it until all the arrangements were made, and then they moved her fast, within a week.

When Donny heard of it a fury rose from within him — a fury he had not thought himself capable of feeling. How could his mother be evicted from her own home, and by her own son? How could Daniel do this without consulting him? She was his mother, too, for heaven's sake! It was unforgivable, and he and Eileen were not going to stand for it. So one Saturday morning they drove into town, picked up his mother, and took her back to their own home, where she lived, hurt and indignant, until she died three years later.

The two brothers never spoke again. Not for thirteen years. Donny stopped coming over to borrow equipment or to pass through on his way to town, and gradually the road through the woodlot grew over. The two children of Donny and Eileen, and the three of Daniel and Margaret, were forbidden to play with their cousins, and they grew up hardly knowing one another. Daniel, who had been having a difficult time anyway adjusting to the new rector at St. Jude's, decided it was time to leave the Anglican Church and went into town to join the Presbyterians.

And that is about where things stood by the time I arrived at St. Jude's. Mrs. Lucas had died years ago. Donny and Eileen came to church from time to time but could hardly be described as active members. I married Sean, their oldest, the first year I was there, but I didn't even know Donny had a brother until the provincial ploughing match the following summer, the year it was held on the old Lucas farm.

I met Daniel on his own turf, with pick-ups and tractor trailers parked the full length of his quarter-mile driveway, John Deeres and Internationals strewn about the west tract, a big hospitality tent set up on his front lawn, and hundreds of farmers in jeans and work boots sipping coffee and trading stories under the loudspeakers. I was young and in my clericals, and I approached Daniel to introduce myself to him. He stood his ground solidly, his feet slightly apart and a wry smile on his lips. He was a big solid man, and my hand felt small in his powerful grasp. But he received me congenially, watching me and weighing my words while not giving away anything himself.

We exchanged small talk for a while. A few others hung back, listening in. He was the host of this gathering, and its undisputed champion. He had won the competition last year and was clearly proud of that, though I'm sure he wouldn't have admitted it in so many words. So, innocently, I told him I hadn't realized he was Donny's brother and that I must have missed him at Sean's wedding. All friendliness drained from his face. Everything went quiet as he fixed me with his eyes. "I wasn't at the wedding," he said curtly. I stammered something vaguely apologetic and then, under the force of that gaze, found a reason to excuse myself.

It was a piece of overheard gossip that finally brought the brothers together again. At the Monday meeting of the Happy Hookers' Craft Guild at the church, Margaret heard a few of the ladies talking in hushed tones out in the kitchen. From the work circle in the other room she could hear them saying what a shame it was, with Donny being so sick and in hospital now.

The next day Margaret looked up from doing the dishes to see Daniel coming down the stairs in his suit jacket, his plaid shirt buttoned up to the neck. He never wore this jacket, not even to church, and he seemed awkward and ill at ease in it. He looked at her and their eyes met. Margaret didn't have to ask him where he was going. "Oh, Dan," she said, and she began to cry. He held her, looking out across the yard, fighting back his own emotion.

I was at the hospital that day, sitting by Donny as he struggled to breathe. He had had a cough that fall that wouldn't go away, and he found himself getting increasingly short of breath. He put it down to the wet weather and to his having put on a few pounds over the last few years. But when suddenly, without trying to, he started losing the weight, but not the cough, Eileen grew worried enough to take him to the doctor. The cancer was all through him by then, and within a week he was hospitalized with two, maybe three, months to live.

Daniel didn't see me at first as he entered the room, his cap in his hand. He walked uncertainly to the other side of the bed. He squinted through his thick eyebrows, trying to recognize this familiar stranger. Donny lay propped up on pillows, his face gaunt and grey, an oxygen mask strapped over his mouth and nose. Daniel looked over and saw me but said nothing. For a few moments there was only the hiss of the oxygen and Donny's short shallow gasps.

Daniel cleared his throat. He pulled a chair up to the bed and sat on its edge. His lip quivered and his eyes began to fill with tears. His mouth moved but no sound came.

At that moment Donny woke up. Struggling to focus, he looked at his brother. He was too weak to speak, but he raised his hand ever so slightly. Daniel took Donny's hand in his, and the two men began to weep.

Donny died a mere six weeks later. At the funeral the two families were together for the first time since Mrs. Lucas's death so many years ago. The cousins chatted easily with each other at the reception back in the church hall, and as the small crowd thinned, the older ones drifted together over to the Legion hall for a beer.

The next spring Daniel recut the road through the woodlot, opening the passage between the two farms. Margaret and Eileen began visiting back and forth. They discovered they shared much in common, including a cache of stories about old Mrs. Lucas. In the lighter moments they would laugh together until their sides ached.

As I write this, all is quiet on the upstairs front. But I think I can hear a door about to open. If I'm right, it's the only door we've been given.

Words

Words are what we have been given. But they are never enough. Not for the really important things.

Preachers are aware of this every week that they rise to the pulpit or wander down the aisle to speak again the Good News. It is an impossible burden. Words of life are called for, yet each week they hear once again coming from their mouths the same hackneyed expressions, the same theological predilections, the same sameness. It has been said that every preacher has only one sermon. And most of us preached it long ago!

Yet the church is crammed to its vaulted ceiling with words. Over the eons they accumulate, packed together shoulder to shoulder like beef calves on their way to slaughter, their feet barely touching the floorboards. They push out against the walls, and centuries-old stained glass bulges with the pressure.

I imagine a curious passer-by, attracted perhaps by the sound of singing, approaching a grand old cathedral late on a Sunday morning. Tentatively he ascends the broad concrete steps rising from the sidewalk. A sound like that of a rushing wind can be heard approaching. Suddenly the heavy oak doors burst open, sending him flying a hundred feet in the air. Wrong place at the wrong time, someone will think as they read about it next day in the paper. But it wasn't location that killed him. It was words, too many words.

There are indications that the world, too, is growing weary of our words. A slogan on a nearby overpass was recently edited to read, "Jesus is Gord!" And would-be vandals, hampered only by their illiteracy, last fall spray-painted a bold message at the doors of our church. "Satin rules," the block letters screamed. The fashion vigilantes had struck again.

But the truth is, however offensive our proliferation of words, however inadequate and cumbersome, the alternative is unthinkable, at least for most Christians. Each week in our worship we try to observe a reflective silence following each of the readings. The idea is that the reader stands quietly at the lectern for a few moments, so that we might allow the word of God to sink in a bit before we move on. But you would think we were asking people to sit through the Christmas recital of the junior violin class.

The readers, like readers everywhere, announce the conclusion of the reading, linger self-consciously for a millisecond and then immediately begin fidgeting with the pages of the large lectern Bible, turning over whole sections at a time, adjusting ribbons. The congregation en masse makes a grab for the pew bulletin to see what's coming up next. Throats are cleared, bodies get readjusted in the pews. People look at their watches and grow impatient. Finally, an agonizing ten seconds later, the silence ends and everyone breathes out with relief.

So I should have known better than to invite a mime to preach the sermon last Sunday. It was one of those impulsive things you do from some deep desire or need you can't quite name. It did not go before the worship committee, as most innovations do in our church. It barely even passed through my own silly ideas detector. But I had been riding high since the success of our Blessing of the Animals service last fall, and she was *so* good doing her busker routine downtown one Saturday morning a few weeks back. My kids were entranced. My wife clapped her hands in sheer delight. And I had a brainwave.

When she had acknowledged the applause of the crowd and passed round a dusty old top hat, the performance seemed to be over. So I approached her. She remained perfectly in character, raising her eyebrows and leaning forward in exaggerated interest. First I told her how much we had just enjoyed the show. She raised a hand over her eyes and turned away, feigning modesty.

I said I was a parish priest. Her fingers parted, and she peeked out at me with guarded interest from behind her hand. It might be ridiculous, I said, but I couldn't help wondering how my congregation would react if she were to give the sermon some Sunday. Obviously the content would have to be less, well, specific than usual. After all, I didn't even know if she had Christian sympathies.

She leaned forward, planting her hands on her knees, and cocked her head in a mixture of amusement and curiosity. I reflected how wonderful it might be for us to "hear" the gospel afresh through someone who didn't use words.

She was staring at me, frozen in a gesture I couldn't read. It was as if she had retreated for the moment to some inner dressing-room while she considered the offer. Even her eyes, behind the thick greasepaint, revealed nothing. Then she was back. In a formal gesture, she straightened up and produced from somewhere a business card. I thanked her and said I would be in touch.

I was excited as we drove home in the car. The kids were ecstatic. Were we really going to have a clown in church? They wouldn't have to go to Sunday school that day, would they? My wife was less certain about the idea. Are you sure the church is ready for this, she asked me. It would be great, I said, just great!

It wasn't until the next Monday that I pulled the card from my wallet to give her a call. I wondered what it would be like to hear her voice. But as I turned the card over in my hand I realized there was nothing on it. I turned it over again. Absolutely nothing. I couldn't believe it! But then again, what did I expect? She was a *mime*, after all.

So this was a puzzle. A business card that was completely blank. How was I to contact her? I made a closer inspection of the card. Nothing. But as I ran my thumb over the surface I thought I could feel something. I held it up to the light. Still nothing. But there was definitely something there, a waxy streak, perhaps a stain of some kind.

I sharpened a pencil and began shading the card lightly. As I did, something in the smell of the wood shavings reminded me in passing of grade school, where a freshly sharpened pencil and a blank piece of white paper were all one needed to open a world of possibilities. Magically, words began appearing on the card. DUMBSTRUCK PRODUCTIONS, it announced, and it gave a phone number. Clever.

When I called I got a taped message. It was not one of those slick automated call-answering programs provided for a fee by the phone company. Nor was it a live answering service. It was an old click-and-whir answering machine. The message was scratchy, but a female voice seemed to be inviting me to leave a message. So at the beep I left my name and number along with the date and time of a Sunday service several weeks hence.

A few days later, when I hadn't heard anything, I left another message, asking someone to please call me to confirm the date. I gave explicit directions how to get to the church and asked if a ride would be needed. I also mentioned that, of course, an honorarium would be provided and apologized for not having made that clear when we spoke. The machine cut me off with a click before I had finished.

The next day, Grace, our church secretary, complained to me that she had been getting crank calls all morning. The caller wasn't saying anything. Grace said she couldn't even hear breathing. So she would just hang up. I told her next time it happened to transfer the call to me. She looked dubious. I reassured her that I thought I knew who it might be and that, if I was right, it was all quite harmless.

Sure enough, about fifteen minutes later the call came, and Grace gave it to me. Covering the mouthpiece, she whispered, "I think this is the call you were waiting for." I said hello, but there came no reply. I said I was grateful for the call and that I would assume it was confirmation of our date. I gave her the readings for the day. I asked if someone would let me know if anything was needed by way of set-up. There was still only silence. I thanked her again and hung up.

Maybe I've been doing this job too long. But I couldn't recall having been so excited about a liturgical event in a very long time. Not even the visit of the lieutenant governor last year had stirred my blood. Sure, it got our picture in the local paper, and he really gave us quite a good little pep talk about loving one another, or something. But in the end, it had all seemed like just a lot of extra work for me.

This was different. Even I didn't know what to expect. And I found myself relishing the suspense when I announced in church that next Sunday at our main service we would have a guest preacher whose name I didn't know and who probably would choose not to speak to us. You'll just have to be here, I teased.

And they were. Nothing like a little mystery to bring people back to church.

Ten minutes before the service my kids — who had entered into the conspiracy and not told a soul — burst into the vestry. "She's here, she's here!" they cried. I went to the back door to see her getting out of a beat-up import.

She was already in costume and make-up. She saw my kids and greeted them with open arms as if she were a visiting relative. They responded as if she were, and rushed into her arms. She tweaked their ears and pinched their noses. They walked together arm in arm across the parking lot, like Dorothy and her friends on their way to Oz.

I put out my hand when they got to the door, but instead of taking it she gave me a low bow. I couldn't but respond in kind. I felt as giddy as a big kid. As I led her to the vestry I began explaining how things worked, where the sermon would come in the service, where she would be sitting. She furrowed her brow deeply and stroked her chin, taking in my words with such exaggerated interest I wondered if indeed she was paying the slightest attention.

Finally I gave up. "You'll see," I said, which seemed a relief to her, and she dragged her sleeve across her brow, wiping the imaginary sweat to the floor.

We met the choir as they were assembling in the narthex. I introduced her as our preacher. She gave a shy curtsy. The choir members stared in amazement. Oh, oh, I thought, as I read their reaction. Gail, one of the younger members, and Bill, a jokester in his own right, both smiled, catching something of the excitement of the moment. But the rest, to a member, reflected only horror and dismay. Oh, my God, I could hear them thinking, what has he done this time?

The organ swelled and the procession began. Our mime, in front of me, took her place like a bridesmaid in a formal wedding, one foot sliding out in front, the other catching up, touching toe to carpet, then sliding out in turn. She held her hands out in front as if clasping a bouquet. Her face was solemn and she looked straight ahead.

The people on the aisles did a double take as they caught their first sight of our guest. Children yanked at their parents' sleeves. Old Mrs. Riley, sitting in her usual place on the aisle, unable to stand along with the rest of the congregation, appeared genuinely delighted as she craned her neck and caught the fantastic sight. This was a good sign.

I ushered the mime to a seat behind the pulpit, the usual place for preachers, and returned to the top of the chancel steps for the greeting. The words were no sooner out of my mouth than I was aware of distracting movement off stage to my right. The mime was standing on her tippy-toes, peering out over the top of the pulpit. Her eyes were wide, her body taut, as she strained to take in the congregation. People were snickering.

I said we had a special guest with us this morning who would be preaching the sermon, so the children were invited to stay with us in church rather than go down to Sunday school. That was when I suddenly realized I had neglected to inform Bonnie, the Sunday school superintendent. She was staring at me, incredulous, from the side door, where she stood ready to usher them all downstairs.

"Oops, sorry," I said aloud. Bonnie returned to her seat, red-faced and fuming. There would need to be a little bridge-mending there.

We got through the collect and the readings without incident, the mime taking in the service with eyes that were wide and alert as she sat at the edge of her seat in the sanctuary. I rose to read the gospel, which I had changed to fit the occasion.

"In the beginning was the Word," I intoned. "And the Word was with God, and the Word was God ..."

But no one seemed to be listening. The mime had risen from her seat and was making her way down the chancel steps. No, I thought, not yet. She was walking slowly, cautiously, up to the first pew.

I tried to continue. "The true light that enlightens everyone was coming into the world ..."

Tentatively, she approached little Devon, a lively four-year-old who often disrupts my children's talks with delightful non sequiturs about his bunny or Spider Man or anything else that happens to cross his mind at the moment. She extended her hand to him, but he slunk back into his mother's side, his eyes glued to the mime. Her hand made a motion in the air as if she was caressing his head. He remained uncertain.

"The world was made through him," I continued, "yet the world knew him not."

She straightened up as she saw Gus, sitting at the end of a pew, his arms folded across his chest, much like he does every Sunday, unmoved by my jokes, unsympathetic to my deepest insights. She folded her own arms across her chest and raised her head to peer down at him. I heard someone chuckle. Gus was not amused, his face folding into a dark scowl. Suddenly she twirled round on her toes, producing from mid-air a bouquet of plastic flowers. She looked at him uncertainly for moment, then tossed them carelessly into his lap.

Her interest was caught by old Mrs. Riley.

"But to all who received him, who believed in his name, he gave power to become children of God ..."

She approached Mrs. Riley up the main aisle as if in the court of a queen. Arriving at her pew, she knelt on one knee before her. She took Mrs. Riley's hand and, raising it slightly, drew it to her lips and kissed it. A broad smile spread across Mrs. Riley's face and, rising fully to the occasion, she gave the mime a regal nod.

And so she made her way down the aisle, greeting each one who caught her eye. I struggled on with the reading. "And from his fullness have we all received, grace upon grace."

Suddenly, from the back of the church, she turned and ran up the aisle. At the chancel steps she stopped, twirled around and stood resolutely with her feet wide apart, her hands on her hips, eying us all. Then she reached deep into her pockets and brought forth handfuls of gold coins, the kind with chocolate inside. With a flourish she tossed them high into the air. There was a gasp from little mouths. The coins landed, hitting people on the head, ricocheting off the backs of pews. Squealing children scrambled to get them.

She reached deeply again, and tossed into the air another handful. She held her arms high, suspended for a dramatic moment, and then reached down again. Jubilant, with the congregation now in chaotic abandon, she skipped down the aisle, showering one side of the church and then the other.

When she reached the back she turned and tossed two more handfuls. Then she looked at me across the distance. It was the first time our eyes had really met. I tried to smile but could feel emotion rising in my throat, a strange combination of gratitude and regret. She took off her top hat and gave me a low slow bow. Then she backed out of the church and left.

For a moment there was delirium, as children leapt over pews, their parents unable to restrain them. After everything had died down, the congregation was breathing hard, a little flushed, and looking up at me in the pulpit. I collected myself and, inspired by the lunacy of it all, simply shrugged my shoulders and returned to my place in the sanctuary.

"And now to God the Father, God the Son, and God the Holy Spirit ..." I began. Everyone rose to their feet instinctively. "... Be ascribed all might, majesty, power, dominion and glory, for ever and ever."

"Amen," came the reply.

Weddings 'R' Us

Father David bent over and planted a kiss on the top of Catherine's head. She didn't look up from her dolls but asked him as he left the room, "You go meeting, Daddy?" He stopped at the door and smiled. "Yes, Daddy go to meeting, sweetie."

He went down the hall and looked in on Paul, who was in the bathtub. "Good night, buddy," he said. "See you in the morning." Paul for some reason was sitting upright in the middle of the tub with a washcloth on his head, one corner dripping down over his eyes and nose. He took it off as his father entered.

"Dad," he said, "why do you go out so much?" "It's my, ah, job, Paul. I've got to meet with some people." "Why don't you meet them in the morning?" Paul asked his dad. "They couldn't see me in the morning," David answered him. For a moment a reflective silence hung between them. "I'll tuck you in when I get home," David offered. "I'll be asleep," Paul reminded him, "but you can wake me up." "Okay. G'night," David said and left the room.

Downstairs in the kitchen Beverley was on the phone, talking to her sister. They were making plans for a family get-together at Christmas. "We can't get away until after lunch, though," she was saying. "David has a service at ten. We could be on the road by one." David got her attention and pointed silently to the church. She gave him a smile and waved with her fingers. He put on his boots and overcoat and quietly closed the door behind him.

It was late November, but already it was feeling like deep winter. The night was black and the frozen earth crunched beneath his feet as he headed across to the church. His white breath hung in front of him in disappearing mists. He pulled up his collar, wishing he had thought to grab his scarf, too.

It was on a night as dark as this that he and Beverley, ten years ago next Wednesday, had leaned into each other as they headed out from their wedding reception, waving good-bye to their family and friends, pointing the headlights toward the highway and their new life together. He realized in passing that he still hadn't bought an anniversary present for her.

His meeting at the church was with a couple he had not met before. The bride-to-be had called earlier in the week, asking to speak with "the Reverend." How much did he charge, she wanted to know, to do a wedding, and was the church booked a certain date a few weeks hence? He had been non-committal, suggesting instead that they meet and talk about it.

Her name was Randi. She and her fiancé, Todd, were waiting in their car in front of the church, the windows frosted up, the heater and the car stereo blasting away from inside as silent white fumes rose from the car's tailpipe into the still air.

In the cramped vestry Father David took his seat opposite them behind his desk. They kept their coats on and leaned forward in the two chairs provided for them, as if perhaps they had left the car running and were expected back at the pool hall any minute.

Father David tried to rise above his weariness and put forward a friendly face, the face of the "welcoming church," to these two youngsters. He asked them how they'd met. "Friends," Todd answered, and they stared ahead at Father David.

"Friends?" he inquired.

"Ya. I was going out with Randi's sister," Todd said, as if that explained everything.

"So, you were going out with Randi's sister," Father David repeated.

"Ya. But I didn't, like, actually meet her until a friend of ours — well, he isn't really a friend, but sort of an acquaintance — like, he had this party? And Randi was sort of going out with him at the time. But he was being a jerk. So I was coming off work, eh? And I guess I'd had a few drinks. So I come to this party, right?"

David hadn't been drinking the night he met Beverley. But the effect was similar. He was a young deacon, an assistant curate at the cathedral. She was a novice in the Anglican Order of St. Cecilia. He had taken the youth group to the convent during the Christmas holidays for a light program of daytime winter sports and evening Bible study. Beverley was assigned to the group, to assist David in leading the evening sessions and to play her guitar for some group singing.

It impressed him that she was so confident with this age group. Her good nature and plump energetic presence provided an infectious atmosphere of holiday cheer, and they all liked her immediately. When David lead the discussion she was attentive, adding illustrations to support what he was saying. How quickly and easily they became a team.

"So, I just looked at her and, like, I knew, right?" Todd was saying. Randi's face, meanwhile, revealed nothing.

"And you, Randi, how did you feel, meeting Todd?" Father David asked her.

"I thought he was kinda cute," she said, without smiling.

The last evening of the retreat David and Beverley gradually took over the discussion themselves as one by one the kids drifted off to their rooms. The two of them were so caught up with one another they hardly noticed them leaving, until a hush fell on the guest-house and it became clear that it was late and they were alone.

They spoke openly about important things, about vocation and family and shared values. By the time they parted, well past midnight, something had passed between them, something that made the leave-taking awkward the next day. Beverley wouldn't look at him directly as she said her good-byes to the group, speaking loudly with a forced gaiety.

There had been some sort of fight, out on the lawn, Todd was explaining. So he asked if she wanted to leave. She did, and that was it.

"That was it?" Father David asked.

"Yup. I guess we've been together ever since," Todd said, looking over at his fiancée.

Three weeks later David received a note from Beverley. It began formally, thanking David for the opportunity of working with him and the young people, and saying how much she had enjoyed them all. But then her words took an unexpected turn.

She wrote that she had especially appreciated the time they had spent together talking that last evening. It had been very refreshing, and she had found herself surprisingly comfortable with him, more comfortable than she had been with anyone else before. This had helped her make a decision she had been wrestling with for some time, a decision about her religious vocation. She had decided not to follow through with the profession of her vows for the time being, but to seek a leave of absence from the Order while she sorted out matters in her own heart and mind.

She was not asking anything of him, she was just letting him know, though she would be pleased to see him if he wanted to. He wanted to.

"So why is it you want to get married?" Father David asked. Todd and Randi looked at him blankly. They didn't seem to have an answer. "I mean, some would consider living together good enough," Father David continued.

"Well, we love each other, right?" Todd answered. "And Randi, like, wants the wedding thing — y'know, the dress and all that."

"It's not just that," Randi cut in, her eyes staring at the carpet in front of her. "I mean, I want that, I've always wanted that. Who doesn't?"

"So, what *is* the reason, Randi?" Father David probed. "What *is* the reason you want to get married?" The two fell silent. Father David began to get the idea. "Are you pregnant?"

David had entered his own marriage a virgin. It was an improbable state for a man his age. Sure, he had performed the requisite blind groping and fumbling on a few dates, but it had never led anywhere. He had begun wondering if perhaps he weren't "manly" enough to be married, though he lacked any natural curiosity for the male body that would have indicated his sexual orientation lay elsewhere.

Beverley was more experienced, but those had not been pleasant experiences. Her buoyant personality had ensured her a measure of popularity at school, but it had also attracted boys who interpreted her easygoing nature as meaning she was simply "easy." More recently she had come to believe that her ruddy face and rotund body precluded any real intimacy with a man, though her own natural curiosity continued to nudge her in that direction.

So their lovemaking had been a wonder-filled revelation to them both. He proved a careful lover, sensitive and patient. She, in turn, offered him adventurous variations on their routine, which proved unnecessary in any case because their shared intimacy was more than enough for him, and he was satisfied.

"Did the two of you talk this out?" Father David asked. "If it weren't for the pregnancy, would you be getting married?"

"Like I said," Todd answered, leaning forward in his chair, "we love each other, man. I mean, like, what are you trying to get at?"

"I'm not trying to get at anything," Father David said, rubbing his forehead with the tips of his fingers. "I'm only asking if you've thought this through. Do you talk, the two of you? Do you have discussions about your relationship, your future together, disagreements maybe? Do you settle your disagreements?"

It amazed David that he and Beverley so seldom fought. He wondered if perhaps this was an unhealthy sign. Normal couples fight. But it didn't feel unhealthy. Somehow they had both carved out their respective areas of responsibility and authority. Beverley ran the home. That was her choice, and she really didn't want her husband interfering too much with the day-to-day operation of the household, which included the budget and the cash flow. He never even saw his pay cheque.

For his part, David was expected to do a share of the chores and, on Saturdays, fix things around the house and yard. Beverley kept a list for this purpose attached by a magnet to the side of the fridge. This meant he could make a contribution without getting underfoot. It also meant that Beverley could become,

without compunction, his most fervent supporter in his ministry, helping out where she could — as a member of the altar
guild and leader of the fledgling youth choir — but never over-
stepping her bounds, the parameters of which they both
instinctively understood.

If theirs was a traditional marriage, that was not a problem
for either of them. They "fit," as their friends had told them on
their wedding day, in speeches that had poked only the gentlest
fun at these two earnest young adults. In deference to their sense
of propriety, the reception had only really perked up after they
had gone, the beer flowing and the music cranking up by
degree. But no one had ever dared tell them this.

"Well, then. Is there anything the two of you wanted to ask
me?" Father David inquired of Todd and Randi, sitting fidgeting
before him.

"So, how much will it cost?" Randi asked him.

Father David's head dropped as he considered the question.
Five thousand dollars would not be too much, he thought. Maybe
ten! That's what they would be spending on the reception, he
was certain.

He could just see it. "And another thing about the bride,"
some school buddy would be slurring, the microphone squealing as he holds onto it for balance. "Another thing you probably
don't know. You know the dugout at the park? And the graffiti
inside? There's, like, one that says ..." The speaker chortles with
glee as if this moment might just be the very apex of his exist-
ence, a roomful of people hanging off his every word. He could
go on like this for hours. And he does.

Father David had seen it all, in the days when he and Beverley
routinely attended wedding receptions. He had watched, horrified, as people entered into lifelong debt for the sake of an outward

show that included an open bar, a chauffeur-driven limousine (perhaps a horse and carriage — Father David had seen that, too), ill-fitting tuxes and bad haircuts, plunging necklines and plastic bouquets. Then a quick drunken departure, a blurred round trip to Hawaii and, when the dazed couple returns, a leather-bound photo album filled with eight-by-ten glossies to recall the whole sordid affair! No, ten thousand dollars would not be too much.

Father David raised his eyes and looked across at them. "It'll cost you a dollar," he said. Todd looked at Randi, disbelieving. Randi looked across at Father David, her dark face uncomprehending. "Though I want you to think about it," Father David added.

"We don't have to think about it," Todd shot back, smiling crookedly. "A buck — really?"

"No, I want you to go home and think about it. Think about what your marriage is worth to you. If it's worth 'a buck,' that's all it will cost you. If it's worth more, then you can give me more. Okay? Think about it."

He closed his file folder and rose from his chair, then extended his hand to each of them in turn, wishing them a good-night.

As he heard the front door of the church close, he went round his desk and reached up to fetch his coat from the hook behind the door. A dull ache was spreading through his lower back. He felt too heavy and slow for a man his age. He left the church, turning off lights and locking doors behind him, and stepped out into the crisp clear night.

The sky above him was brilliant with stars, lively and winking down at him, stretching almost to the horizon on all sides. Across the road in the rectory a light went on in an upstairs window. That would be Beverley getting ready for bed. He stood in the stillness for a moment, gazing across at the house until his eyes began to water with the cold. Then he pulled up his collar and headed for home.

Where Your Treasure Is

When Jesus asked, when did we visit him in prison, it's easy to imagine winos and bikers and teenaged riff-raff, born to the city streets, robbed of better opportunities, mired in pitiable choices and their tragic consequences. Yes, I had thought as a young seminarian, I could see the face of Christ in these my unfortunate brothers. I could even imagine the dank smell of mould and urine stinging my nostrils in the prison corridor, a single light-bulb swinging high overhead.

What I could not have foreseen was the face of Christ in Scott, my rector's warden, peering sadly from behind the polished bars of the holding cell in our swish suburban police station, painted in appealing decorator tones of pearl and roseroot. I would not have imagined having to talk with the desk sergeant about his release, nor witnessing the tearful reunion between Scott and Carolyn, his wife. And all over misplaced treasure.

Scott had started the week in the doghouse. Carolyn had been telling him she wished he'd be more helpful around the house, like, *really* helpful, not just doing these little compulsive jobs he gets in his head that only end up causing more work for her, jobs like, oh, the spot-cleaning of carpets, to name just one.

She pointed out that in reality, he was just having fun, doing the things that gave him personal pleasure, while leaving all the thankless grunt work to her. They both had full-time jobs, but who routinely did the shopping, ran the laundry through, cleaned the bathrooms, scoured the stove top, washed the windows, and arranged the service calls? Did he really think these were things she enjoyed?

He thought this over for a couple of days and couldn't help conceding that he was, in fact, cornered. But the problem was, deep in his soul he really didn't want to do those jobs. He'd grown up the youngest in a family of women, where those jobs just got done. He'd been trained to keep his room tidy and to make his bed and, every so often, to help with the dishes. But he was not a grit and elbow-grease kind of guy. He *could* do those things, he supposed, but not if there was a way out. So he came up with what seemed to him a brilliant compromise, a strategic counter-offensive.

He waited for his moment, which arrived one evening after supper as he joined Carolyn at the dishwasher, a dirty pot in each of his helpful hands. He said casually, "So I thought I'd start making dinner once a week." Carolyn looked at him. "I've been thinking about what you were saying the other day, and I think this might be a way of my making more of a contribution around here. So, Saturday will be my day. I'll plan the menu, do the shopping myself, prepare the meal. It would give you a break."

She placed both hands on the edge of the sink, looking down. He was pleased with himself. This wasn't going to be as hard as he thought.

"You don't get it, do you?" she said.

"Get what?" he said.

"Scott, I *like* cooking. It's one of the things I enjoy. I like going to the market, seeing what's fresh, turning over a few cumquats in my hand, coming up with an original menu. I like chilling the wine, washing the lettuce leaves, slicing the mushrooms, seasoning the sauce. Those are things I *like* doing, Scott, and Saturday is the only day I can do them. So, thanks, but no thanks."

Scott was standing in the middle of the kitchen. He did not move as she took the pots from his hands, placed them in the lower rack of the dishwasher, shut and locked the door tight, started it up, and walked out of the room.

He could feel an emotion rising within him, but he wasn't quite sure which one it was, all of them sort of starting out the same way. He only knew this was a game in all likelihood he could not hope to win. He turned and followed Carolyn down the hall. "Okay, so I'm having a bit of difficulty with this. Maybe I need some help here. I thought the dinner thing would be something I could do, but that's fine. So give me a hand — what *would* be helpful?"

Carolyn was halfway up the stairs. She stopped and thought about this for a moment. "Do you want to know what would be really helpful?" she asked, turning to look down at him. "You could go through your stuff in the attic and get rid of the junk. I know it's important to you, but the thing is, it's been driving me crazy for years. I mean, it's followed us through two apartments, the townhouse and now here it is, still with us. Just throw some of it out. Like the books. You're never going to pick up your old biology textbooks again. And the clocks. Not one of them works. And, Scott? That old steering wheel? Really, it's got to go."

"All right," Scott said, with more enthusiasm than he was actually feeling, "I can do that. Next week is Trash Day anyway. I'll go through it and put whatever I can on the curb. I can do that, that's okay."

She might just as well have asked him to cut off his right arm, but he knew peace is sometimes bought at just such a price. So he spent most of Saturday sitting on the attic floor, sifting through the bits and pieces, saying good-bye to those portions of his past life.

The books were not really so hard to set aside, though he thumbed through them for the little pencilled notes he'd written in the margins. It had been such a novelty to get to that stage in your education where the books are no longer provided by the school. You didn't have to tolerate some bonehead's crude ink drawings or the scribbled phone numbers of people you would never know. Every mark on a page, every nick in a binding, you put there yourself. They were signs of ownership, proof of possession, as good as a bill of sale but written in your own handwriting.

The clocks, he realized, had been a dumb idea to begin with. He had been rummaging through garage sales over the years, collecting windable alarm clocks, not so much for their aesthetic value — he was not a collector *per se* — but as an investment in a future hobby. At a young age he had begun preparing for his retirement, and for some reason clock repair had seemed like a good thing for a retired guy to do. Now, at thirty-six years old, it seemed he had already gathered wisdom enough to realize that broken clocks would hold little interest for him thirty years hence.

The steering wheel, though, that would be a problem. It had absolutely no material value, not even at a wreckers, being bent and tarnished with the leather wrap torn away. It was from the first love of his life, a 1968 MGB-GT, the hatch-back model. He'd picked it up, through an ad in the paper, for a mere $600. The electrical system would cut out every time it rained, and you could see daylight through the rocker panels. But it was a duel carburetor clean-running sleek-lined sports car, so unlike the sensible cars he'd owned since. Until the accident.

It was late at night in the midst of a bad snowstorm, the kind that muffles the city and makes everything appear dreamlike. He must have been dreaming a little himself, because he was on his way home from the library when she started sputtering and then just died on the spot, gliding to a full stop in the middle of the express lanes of the cross-town twelve-lane highway. And it was then that he had the sickening realization that the thing he'd been trying to remember from earlier in the day as he had driven to the university was that, with the gas gauge not working, he should be sure to fill her up on his way home.

He sat in nonplussed silence until a transport roared by, shaking the car and waking him up to the fact that he was sitting in the midst of a very present danger. He grabbed his briefcase from the passenger seat, but as he turned to reach for his tuque in the back-seat, his face was lit by oncoming headlights. He leapt from the car and made it to the shoulder in time to see her rear-ended by a common sedan. There was the sound of shattering glass and crunching metal and the MGB shot silently forward on the road's icy surface. She glanced off the guard rail on the other side and glided back across all three lanes, spinning around twice, striking the concrete abutment before coming to rest a hundred feet down the road.

She was a write-off. But Scott visited her at the pound before letting her go, removing the steering wheel as a memento. The snow crunched underfoot and the cold air hurt his lungs as he walked away from her for the last time.

But it was still true that, looking at it now, the wheel itself had little to commend it. It took up space, was certainly not mountable, and retained little actual interest for him in itself. Carolyn was right. It ought to go.

Trash Day came along twice a year in Scott and Carolyn's neighbourhood, once in the fall, when the focus was on leaves and brush, and again in the spring, when discarded metal objects seemed to be the dominant theme — chrome tables and chairs, stoves and dryers, bicycles, lawnmowers — along with the usual bundles of books and magazines and twisted outdoor toys.

The neighbourhood became creepy in the days just before the official trash removal. As evening fell, the trim streets with their precise lawns and crew-cut hedges were transformed into a scavenger's harvest, small pick-ups and old station-wagons creeping noiselessly along, slowing at each driveway, sometimes stopping, someone pulling a bedframe from a pile, lashing it roughly to the roof, then silently slipping back into the night, the have-nots panning for gold among the cast-offs of the haves, seeing treasure where only refuse was before — iron fireplace grates, curtain rods, sofas, and table lamps.

Do not lay up for yourselves treasures on earth, Jesus said, where moth and rust consume and thieves break in and steal. But this is harder than it sounds, especially when your earthly discards become fortune in the eyes of others.

Watching TV with Carolyn on Monday night, Trash Day eve, Scott was distracted, thinking of the small unprotected pile of stuff he had placed at the curb before supper. He had made a bit of a show of it for Carolyn, chronicling what he had decided to part with, and why. He had taken things out of boxes and brought them to her, saying, "So I figured these could go. I haven't used them for years, and I'm not likely to in the near future." "That's great, Scott," she had answered, looking up as a mother might glance at her child's latest crayon masterpiece.

But of all the stuff that had ended up at the curb, it was the steering wheel that nagged him the most. He knew it had no value; he knew it was only sentiment that had made him hang onto it these twenty years. He knew he could not justify keeping it. And yet it nagged at him, his steering wheel sitting out there alone among the textbooks, the rusted camp stove, the jars of misfitting nuts and bolts. Pouring himself another Scotch, he tried to watch the images passing before him on the screen.

He rose from his chair. "I'm just going to check on the stuff outside," he announced to Carolyn. "Okay, hon," she said.

He went to the living-room window and parted the sheer curtains. A dark vehicle was parked at the curb. A long-haired man with a handlebar mustache was rummaging through his stuff. He watched as the stranger pulled out the steering wheel, holding it up to the light of the street lamp for inspection.

Scott's legs started moving before he had even made up his mind. He was out the front door in his T-shirt and bedroom slippers and heading down the front walk as the man tossed the wheel on the back of his flatbed pick-up, atop a mound of sewing machines and plumbing parts.

"Hey, excuse me," Scott called out. "I'm sorry, that's not for sale. I mean, I'm not throwing that out."

The man didn't seem to hear him. He got back into the truck and started off down the street.

"HEY!" Scott yelled, surprised by the force of his own voice. "Come back here!" Scott ran down the street after him, waving his arms. "Hey! You've got something of mine there!" The truck sped up.

"Damn," Scott muttered as he stopped where he was. He considered his options, then raced back to the house and grabbed his keys from their hook inside the front door. His hands were shaking as he fumbled with the ignition. He threw the Tercel into reverse and swung onto the street, backing over the curb, his rear wheel coming down with a thunk. He headed off in search of the thief. Where would he have gone? Was he still cruising the neighbourhood or had he already headed for the highway?

He decided to try the street behind his and Carolyn's. Other older vehicles were creeping along, plying their shameless trade. He passed them a little faster than was safe. At the cross street he thought he'd make a detour to the main thoroughfare, which led to the entrance ramp to the highway. He could park by the gas station, knowing at some point this guy had to go home. But just as he was starting into his turn he saw brake lights up ahead in the next block. It was his man.

Scott pulled the car up close behind him and got out. "I'm sorry, but you've taken something of mine," he said. The man was bending down, reaching for a set of chrome table legs. "I don't think so," he replied, not looking up.

"A steering wheel," Scott went on. "It doesn't have any value to you, it's worthless. I didn't mean to throw it out."

"But you did, didn't you?" The man straightened up and looked Scott over. This seemed to give him confidence. "You did throw it out, didn't you!" he said again. "And I got it, don't I!"

Scott could feel himself getting angry. His stomach was quivering. This was what he all his life had tried to avoid. He hated confrontation. It frightened him, though not so much the threat of being hurt as the rising of his own inner rage, the release of his own demons.

"That steering wheel has sentimental value to me," Scott said emphatically. "You're not just going to walk away with it!"

The man threw the table legs into the back of his truck, walked to the cab, climbed in, and began driving off.

"Oh, no, you don't," Scott hissed through his teeth. He jumped into the car and stepped on the gas, roaring its little motor up behind the truck and screeching to a stop inches from the thief's rear bumper. The truck slowed and then picked up speed again. Again Scott tore up to him, this time bumping the truck's read fender. Both vehicles came to a stop in the middle of the street. The man flew out of the cab, then reached for something in the back. He approached Scott, wielding a tire iron.

"You give me back that steering wheel," Scott said, "or, God help me, I'll plough right into you!" For a moment it was a stand-off.

"You want it?" the man snarled, finally. "Then go get it!"

He reached into the back of the truck, found the steering wheel, and then flung it as hard as he could high into the air. It sailed like a frisbee overhead, striking the TV antenna atop the house across the street, bouncing off the roof into some bushes below. The man stared at Scott for a moment, sizing up whether this neat yuppy type, standing half in, half out of his Toyota in his bedroom slippers, was a fighter. Risking he was not, he threw the tire iron into the back of the truck, got in, and drove off.

Scott parked the car by the curb, turned the headlights off, then ventured into the darkness between the houses to find his wheel. The bushes were some kind of overgrown prickly shrub that filled the space between the one house and the backyard fence of its neighbour. He leaned into the darkness, reaching way down deep, then lost his balance and tumbled headfirst into the thorny bramble.

Still he could not locate the wheel. He got himself upright and edged his body between the house and the brush, scraping his back along the brick, feeling his way in with one hand, guarding his face against the thorns with the other. Some small rodent at his feet scurried away as he wedged himself in deeper, groping for the elusive treasure.

He was suddenly interrupted by a single beam of light shining through the darkness, reflecting off the rim of the wheel, which he saw was only a foot or so away. He made a grab for it, but a voice called out, stopping him.

"You there, come out slowly, and no funny business!" The voice had authority. He turned his head toward the light and could see, behind it, the unmistakable shape of a police cruiser. Blinded by the direct beam of the flashlight, he struggled to free himself from the nettles. He emerged backward onto the front lawn and turned to face two police officers and an older woman in a bathrobe.

When they asked him why he had been yelling at the house, why he had tried to destroy this woman's TV antenna, and why he was breaking into her backyard, they didn't have patience to hear the story he tried to tell them, not when they smelled the liquor on his breath.

The one call permitted him was to me. He recalled that I had been made volunteer chaplain to the local police detachment a couple of years ago. I was to tell Carolyn what had happened and see if I could do anything to set things right with the police.

Fortunately, it turned out that I knew the desk sergeant. It was clear the police were not regarding Scott as a threat to public safety, but thought a few hours in the holding cell might just sober him up to the reality of his having just disturbed the peace. They let him go with a warning, but not before Carolyn arrived.

She was at first incredulous. How could this have happened? But as Scott told his story, a smile spread across her face. She hid it with her hand at first, but couldn't stop herself. She started to laugh. "Oh, Scott," she said, hooking her arm in his as they left the station, "it's a good thing I love you."

A bird in the hand, I couldn't help thinking, as I watched them get into her car and head for home.

Jim Thompson's Seder

By the time I got out of bed the day had already started without me. I had forgotten until I gazed out the kitchen window that the car was in for repairs, and I had to be downtown at the synod office by nine for the first meeting of a new committee I was supposed to be on. That meant skipping breakfast, yanking my "slush rubbers" up over my shoes under a slew of muttered oaths, and heading out to catch the first in a series of lumbering fumy public transportation vehicles that would eventually land me downtown fifteen minutes late — if I was lucky. My wife would call ahead to let them know I was on my way.

I had not been thrilled when the bishop appointed me to the new Inter-Church Committee on Affordable Housing, or ICCAH, which people were already using as a proper noun, as in, " Ikka should talk to the folks at Oopa" (meaning, the Urban Planning Association, or UPA).

The committee's heady purpose was to launch a coordinated attack on urban homelessness by building affordable housing units in strategic locations throughout the downtown core. There was seed money from three levels of government, cooperation from other denominations, and several social agencies offering their expertise. So what was *I* doing there? I didn't have two acronyms to rub together.

It wasn't that the cause was unworthy of me; quite the opposite: I felt unworthy of the cause. I am a priest and a pastor. I have no expertise in the social ministries. And, quite frankly, the clergy who do make me nervous. They are so intense about it, so righteously indignant at the state of the world, that they end up making everyone else feel guilty, especially those of us living and ministering in the cushy suburbs.

It is my parishioners, after all, who clog the parkways and pollute the air with their single-passenger sedans; who fill the anonymous office towers with their insatiable need for more parking space, more hydroelectric power, more handball courts; who brush past the shopping carts of homeless people while on the way to their power lunches; who then *en masse* at the end of the day turn their backs on the city for their comfortable homes and gardens, leaving the police, the social agencies, and a few ill-attended under-funded downtown churches to deal with whatever refuse gets left behind.

Not that these clergy say this to your face. But they think it. And now I was going to be one of them. Maybe riding public transportation to the meeting today would help. Maybe I should have worn the shirt that was fraying at the collar. In any case, I thought I'd better just keep my mouth shut for a while until I got the lay of the land — or, of the street, as the case may be.

I pulled my collar up against the mid-winter chill and looked across the bus at the dishevelled person sitting opposite me. He was hunched forward, looking down at the floor, his feet spread, taking up both seats. His gnarled hands clutched a brown paper sack, the kind with twine loops for handles. The sack seemed to contain nothing but plastic bags, scrunched together and filthy.

He wore several layers of clothing, including a top coat that resembled my own, several decades from now, and a pair of cast-off loafers, the stitching gone at the toes, wrenched over thick wool socks. I noticed that from beneath his pant cuffs, frayed and black with grime, there protruded the unmistakable hems of a pair of striped blue pajamas. My breathing stopped.

I was suddenly caught up in a mind-movie, a recollection of an event from my early ministry, so deeply buried I had not thought of it for probably twenty years. It felt like someone's description of a near-death experience where, bathed in light, the events of one's life flash before them and they feel again all the emotions connected with a former time. The reel began to roll from some dark inner projection booth. I was held captive, powerless to stop it.

In the second year of my divinity studies I had been assigned for my field placement to a large suburban church. It was in an old suburb, not far from downtown, on the edges of the university campus. The houses were brick and stone and, inside, graced with the craftsmanship of another era — sculpted plaster mouldings, hand-rubbed woodwork, marble entranceways.

The rector, Brandon Fuller, was a former insurance company executive who kept watch over his parish in grey flannels and a dark blue blazer, like the commandant of a navy vessel. He liked to run a smooth operation from a safe distance. So when new ideas were called for, especially those involving risk of failure, he depended upon his young clergy assistants. That's how it fell to me and Charlie, his twenty-eight-year-old assistant curate, to run that year's Maundy Thursday Seder Supper.

The parish had never had a Seder before. But Mr. Fuller was concerned about declining numbers at Easter and wanted to put some life back into Holy Week. Plus, he had just returned from a tour of the Holy Land, and was wearing a new appreciation for our Jewish roots.

So Charlie and I put our heads together and soon got excited about the possibilities. Jesus, after all, was Jewish, a fact overlooked by most Christians. Whatever the Last Supper was, whether the Passover or a less formal fellowship meal, Maundy Thursday was a great opportunity to point people back to our Jewish roots from which the early church had sprung.

We decided to make it a worship service in two parts. First we would meet over in the church hall for the Proclamation of the Word, a Seder meal, and a pot luck supper. This would provide some new links in our understanding of the eucharist, the second part of our service, which would take place in the church. The evening would be concluded with the solemn stripping of the altar in preparation for Good Friday.

It was brilliant. And Mr. Fuller himself seemed pleased as we explained it all to him at the staff meeting the next week. It would need lots of publicity, though, he warned, because it was something new. But he thought it sounded just the right notes with which to enter the Easter weekend.

So Charlie and I went ahead and planned the whole thing, billing it as a "family night" and emphasizing the pot luck aspect in particular, because at least people would understand what *that* part meant. Our efforts were rewarded when the day came and people began pouring in at the appointed hour — fathers in their grey suits straight from the office, mothers with toddlers, seniors in small clutches, but also, I was alarmed to notice, a stranger who clearly didn't fit any of those categories; in fact, someone I had never seen before, a street person.

Damn! We had gone to a lot of work for this event. Mr. Fuller wouldn't want any trouble. I walked over to the man.

He was definitely from the street. His grey hair and beard were long and matted. He wore a frayed sports jacket over a sweater and several bulky layers beneath that. His baggy pants, secured by a piece of rope around his waist, were khaki Army and Navy Supplies, and he carried under his arm an old gym bag missing its handles.

"Hello," I offered tentatively, more a query than a greeting.

"Hello," he returned. Then, sizing me up and figuring I was bearing some sort of authority, he added, "I saw your notice in the paper and thought I'd just come along."

"Great," I said. "Shit!" I thought.

His face was deeply lined but was not threatening or unkind. He said his name was Jim, Jim Thompson, and he produced from a threadbare wallet an employee's card from CN Rail with a name and picture on it. The picture was of someone unrecognizable from the figure that stood before me, a clean-shaven middle-aged man with a glint in his eye. "I was a railway man," he said.

"Well, thanks for coming, Jim," I said.

By the time I got to Charlie he had already taken care of the situation. Mr. Fuller was apprised and would address it at the appropriate time, which turned out to be in his opening remarks. He strode to the centre of the stage and welcomed everyone without using the microphone, his bellowing voice reaching the noisy corners of the room. As everyone quietened down, he commended

Charlie and me for our work in preparing this very special event in the life of our parish. He hoped everyone would enjoy the evening.

And because part of the Seder tradition is to provide hospitality to the sojourner, the stranger in our midst — Charlie and I looked at one another — Mr. Fuller was particularly pleased to welcome a newcomer, an "urban traveller," who was with us tonight, Mr. Jim Thompson. "Welcome to you, sir," Mr. Fuller boomed across the room. Charlie and I smiled at each other. Smoothie.

Jim had taken a seat at the far end of one of the long tables that were set up at right angles to the walls. When he heard his name, he smiled at everyone and gave a jovial wave. People around him strained to return the smile in his general direction, pulling their children closer.

The proceedings then began with a Hebrew song, which I led on the guitar. "Pray for the peace of Jerusalem, Jerusalem my home," I sang. "Pray for the peace of Jerusalem, Jerusalem, shalom." As I launched into the rousing chorus, people began to clap their hands and move slightly from side to side with the music.

Each table had been set with the symbolic foods of the Jewish Passover. Charlie explained their significance one by one: the roasted lamb, the *haroses* (a mixture of fruit, nuts, and honey), the parsley, and the bitter herbs. A bottle of red wine stood on each table, and we were instructed to fill our juice glasses for the toast, filling one additional glass "for Elijah."

The blessing of the wine, recited by Mr. Fuller, his eyes closed, his voice rising and falling with dramatic license, was likely the very blessing used by Jesus himself as he sat with his friends at the Last Supper: "Blessed art Thou, O Lord God, King of the Universe, Creator of the fruit of the vine, who hast chosen us among all peoples for thy service and hast made us sharers in the blessing of thy holy festivals."

All toasted and drank. I stole a glance at Jim Thompson. He seemed to be settling in and having a wonderful time, toasting and drinking along with his new table family.

Then the bread was broken, a large pita, which Mr. Fuller lifted high into the air and tore in one strong action down the middle. "Lo, this is the poor bread of affliction which our fathers ate in the land of Egypt," his voice boomed. "Let all who are hungry and in want come and celebrate with us."

Table groups broke the bread for distribution. Again I glanced at Jim. He caught my eye with a twinkle that made him look for an instant like a jubilant Santa Claus. He winked at me as he raised a fresh glass of wine, Elijah's probably.

But how right, I thought, that Jim should have joined us this night. How providential, even. I had not really noticed that element in the Seder as we had prepared it, that it was a sign of hospitality to all who suffer, to all who are on the road, because of the restless suffering of God's chosen people.

But I did not have long to ponder this. The program was moving right along and next, before the pot luck was to start, was the *horah*, which I was to lead. I went to the centre of the room, in front of the serving tables laden with casseroles and garlic bread, and showed everyone the basic steps to this traditional Jewish dance. I had everyone hold hands as we walked through it slowly.

Then Charlie put on the tape and we began moving awkwardly forward, then back, then forward again around the serving table, a circle of people joined hand to hand, kicking each other in the shins. The music gathered momentum, and so did we. We were having fun, which was the point, and faces were flushed as people lost their inhibitions and swooped down with enthusiasm into each new movement.

But as the circle wound around the centre of the room, I became aware that Jim was not among us. At the far end, where a serving counter divided the church hall from the kitchen, Jim was helping himself to the desserts, stuffing cupcakes and squares into his jacket pockets. This is okay, I thought, this is as it should be. And we laughed and danced around the table of plenty.

Finally we all lined up on both sides of the serving table and began filling our plates with food. There was no shortage of anything, a fact not overlooked by Jim, his plate piled high. For this brief time the indomitable sea had parted and he was one of us, escaping persecution and on his way to a land overflowing with milk and honey.

But later, in the church, after we had heard again Jesus' poignant words of institution and had made our communion, the altar was stripped, a veil placed over the cross, and the door of the tabernacle left open to expose its emptiness. We were entering the dark eve of Good Friday and, thus instructed, everyone departed in silence.

In the sacristy, hanging up our vestments, Mr. Fuller thanked us again for our efforts. "A very fine evening indeed," he said. "Now, about this fellow … he'll have to leave, of course. Good night, boys."

Neither of us had given any thought to Jim Thompson leaving. I guess we just assumed he'd go away like the rest. But Mr. Fuller was right. We found Jim milling about the corridor by the coat racks. He seemed to be fidgeting with his gym bag.

"Good night, Jim," I said. "It was good to have you with us."

"Oh, it was nice to be here all right," he said. "This is a nice place you've got. I don't suppose you'd mind my just staying here for a while. It's pretty cold out there."

"Sorry, Mr. Thompson," Charlie said, an affected authority in his voice that didn't quite take. "We can't allow that."

"Why not?"

"Well, there are lots of reasons. Insurance and things like that. What if something went missing? You wouldn't want to take the blame for that, would you?"

"You think I'm gonna steal something?"

"No." Charlie was trying to come up with an explanation, any explanation, it didn't matter, just so long as we got him out without any unpleasantness. "No, it's just that you don't want to be responsible if something happens."

"Well, I think I'll just stay here, anyway," Jim replied, looking around for a place to settle down. He entered a pew and dropped his bag on the seat.

"I'm sorry," Charlie tried again, "but everyone else has left, and you have to go, too."

Mr. Thompson was ignoring him.

"Look, Jim, we don't want to have to call the police," I said. I reached for his elbow to guide him in the direction of the door. He shook me off and sat down in the pew. Pulling his bag onto his lap he occupied himself with its contents.

Charlie and I looked at one another. He tilted his head, raising his eyebrows as if to say, "We have no choice." We approached him together. Leaning into the pew from the aisle we reached out to take his arm, but as we did he pulled his legs up and lay down on the pew as if settling for the night. Intuitively agreeing upon our next move, we grabbed his pant legs. Jim rolled over partway and reached for the back of the pew and held on.

"Come on now, Mr. Thompson," Charlie pleaded. "We don't want to have to hurt you." I wondered what he meant. Hit him with a hymn book? We pulled again at his legs, but he flipped himself over onto his back, his chin in his chest, breathing hard through his nose. One hand was wrapped around the back of the pew, the other around the pew in front of him. He was ready for a struggle.

"Okay, Jim," I said, "that's it. You've got to go." But as we gave one last pull at his legs, his belt gave way like a wound spring and his pants slid off into our hands over a pair of striped blue pajama bottoms. Charlie and I were sent flying backward into the aisle.

I don't know which of us was more startled, Charlie or me, but as we sat up and looked at each other we started to laugh. It just struck us as so absurd, the curate and the divinity student yanking off a man's pants in the House of God.

As we pulled ourselves together, Jim Thompson was getting to his feet. He retrieved his pants and put them back on, securing them once again around his waist with the rope belt. From his gym bag he produced a wool tuque and pulled it down over his ears. Slowly, deliberately, he wrapped his jacket around him, tucked his bag under his arm and, without a word, began making his way to the door. I stood up, my face straightening, and watched him go.

Whatever indignity he had just suffered at our hands, it was not him who was shamed that night, and we all knew it as he glanced back one last time before disappearing into the cold night.

"I'm sorry," I said softly after him.

The dishevelled man sitting across from me on the bus looked up. I stared back at him blankly. "I'm so sorry."

My hand groped for my briefcase, and I rose as if still in a dream and made my way to the exit doors. I stepped down from the bus, then stood on the sidewalk for a moment, trying to get my bearings. The bus pulled away, belching its noxious fumes. Slowly, I began walking, my rubbers splish-splashing carelessly through the slush.

At first I didn't know how to feel. I didn't really know what had just happened to me. But then I realized my gait was not heavy; it was light. A quirky smile broke across my face. From somewhere across the star fields of time, had I just received a message? Was this my commissioning for the new work I was about to begin? Did I now get a second chance?

With Jim Thompson's weathered face before me, my stride lengthened. I saw the synod office up ahead. "Thank you, Lord," I whispered, as I reached for the door. "And thank you, Jim, wherever you are."

Powers and Principalities

Gentle Jesus, meek and mild. That was the image given us, growing up, and mostly we believed it.

Jesus, the indefatigable parent, always patient, always wise. Unlike with our real parents, if we messed up with Jesus, it was likely not because *he* was having a bad day. Crayons mixed in with a load of white shirts, caps left off pop bottles in the fridge, the cat's litter box left unchanged for a month — these things would not phase our Lord. He would surely smile understandingly and say, "Let the little children come to me, and do not stop them; for it is to such as these that the kingdom of God belongs." And we would climb up onto his lap, the chocolate on our fingers smearing across his starched white robes.

It was later, in our teens, that this image began to crack. Not even the Son of God can withstand the sullen criticalness of a fifteen-year-old. So, we asked, when Jesus cursed the fig tree, wasn't that swearing? And what's this part here, the part you skipped over, where Jesus made a whip out of cords and drove the moneychangers from the temple, overturning their tables? Did God the Father, like, send him to his room or something? Smirk, smirk.

But in most people's minds, it is still gentle Jesus, meek and mild, not only white but specifically English, who won out. This Jesus would never start a fight, would never talk back to his parents, never make waves. Like most of us, he is too nice for that sort of thing.

Which is too bad, because this Jesus would never presume to step forward to inherit the kingdom promised by the Father, let alone possess the moxie to rule it. This Jesus stands aside at the slightest hint of conflict, docile and subservient to the bullies and antagonists, the schemers and usurpers, who grab the wheel and steer the good ship Ecclesia ever closer to the rocks, jerking the controls from the hands of nice young men or women — many of us clergy — too polite to object, too servile to challenge. We turn and skulk away to our cabins below decks, embarrassed, smiling reassuringly to the crew who lower their eyes as we pass.

But we know that's not the way it's supposed to be. We can almost hear a new rendition of that old Kenny Rogers' tune:

But somethin' always told me we was readin' Jesus wrong:
sometimes you gotta fight when yer God's man.

Deirdre Somerset is known by all at rural St. Jude's, my former parish, as Deedee. It was the name given her when she was a cute blonde high school bombshell some fifty years ago. Her hair remains a respectable platinum approximation of its former glory, with never so much as a strand out of place. She wears smart colour-coordinated ensembles, even when setting up for the rummage sale, and has the same sweet smile for everyone, even as she bosses them around.

At times you can still see traces of the wide-eyed teenaged face, and hear in her laugh that cheerleader giggle. But she is a woman who gets what she wants, usually with the help of that smile, but also with the backing of the entire football team if necessary.

Deedee and Doug, her husband, are not locals. They moved to the area when Doug took early retirement, buying a Better Homes and Gardens converted ski chalet atop ten acres of rolling forested countryside.

Nor was Deedee the natural heir to the altar guild throne. But her timing was impeccable. Vi Hannen was ready to step down as president and, as local tradition dictates, the guild members, out of respect, declined to rush in right away to fill the void. So Deedee was right there to offer a helping hand, having done altar guild work for years down in the city, embroidering linens, arranging flowers, polishing brass — a real workhorse. Like daisies before a steamroller, helpless and quivering, they all lay down and let her roll over them to assume the top job. Her terms quickly established the new regime.

First, the altar guild would become the *chancel* guild. In one fell swoop this increased tenfold the actual square footage of the group's domain. Where before the work had focused on the sanctuary, with its altar and credence table, it now took in the choir stalls, the organ, the lectern, the pulpit, and all antependia in between.

Then Deedee announced she would like to be known not as president of the guild, but as its *directress*. "Presidents" call elections, set agendas, and chair meetings. A "directress" wages war and plots military campaigns, commanding vast armies and taking no prisoners.

The transformation was all but complete by the time I was appointed to St. Jude's, fresh-faced and eager, finally given charge of my own parish. All that remained was to get the new rector onside. So on my first Sunday Deedee stepped up to me, put out her hand, introduced herself, and said she would like me to meet with her at the church next Saturday morning at nine a.m. We needed to "go over a few things," she said. I might have assumed she wanted to know how the new rector wanted things done. It was, of course, the reverse.

When the appointed hour came, she greeted me in the narthex and led me by the arm on a tour of the church. The sacristy was little more than a closet containing an old bedroom bureau with candles and linens in the upper drawers, hangings in the lower drawers. In an old Eaton's department store box, wrapped in tissue and plastic, was a faded brocade superfrontal from the early days of the church, a genuine antique that probably ought to have been displayed under glass. Deedee stuffed it in the box and slid it back under the bureau with her foot.

As she led me around the church, she took special care to point out the various memorials, who had given what, when, and in whose memory. Most seemed to have been fairly recent. Then, with an exaggerated display of reverence, she ushered me into my own vestry and brought out the Book, a leather-bound portfolio listing all the memorials, one to a page, beautifully handprinted in Gothic calligraphy. Deedee had provided the book herself and made each entry: "Burse and Veil in Green: a gift from the Bolton family to the glory of God and in loving memory of Edith Bolton, 1911 – 1984;" "Two brass vases: in loving memory of Charles Gordon, 1919 – 1940."

The Book was important to the people here, she said. She explained this to me carefully, looking at me so hard I had to divert my eyes. Every year it was the custom to bring up the Book in procession at the parish anniversary service. This did not seem to be a suggestion.

I left our meeting feeling strangely weakened, as if suddenly smitten by illness, or perhaps having just witnessed a train wreck. I needed to sit down when I got home and didn't do much for the rest of the day. I was too young to be able to read the signs and to realize I was about to walk into my first tryst not with flesh and blood but with the authorities and powers of this present darkness, with the spiritual forces of evil in the heavenly realms. It was a battle I would lose.

Several months later we began planning the upcoming parish anniversary service. Sitting at the long wooden folding table with the members of the advisory board, I ventured a personal opinion. That part of the service where we process the memorial book, while certainly meaningful and not wholly inappropriate to the occasion, still tended to favour certain members of the congregation, namely, those who could afford to make substantial gifts to the church. For the sake of the justice issues this raised, I said, wandering deeper into the dark woods, perhaps we should not be drawing such inordinate attention to those with means while possibly passing over the "poor widow's mite."

The room fell silent. People looked down at the table. Only Deedee was looking at me. She smiled a sweet forgiving smile. "Thank you for the thought," she said. I felt a sudden chill as a door slammed in my face.

After the meeting I consulted with my churchwardens. Was I out of line, I asked them. Was this so sacred a tradition? It wasn't that, they explained to me. It was more that Deedee had done a great deal since becoming head of the altar guild. She had in a short time procured many donations for the memorial fund, and the church was better off for it. Had I noticed the new silver chalice and patten? That was a memorial Deedee had brought in. She had saved the church a lot of money, though no one could say exactly how much, because the memorial money was run through the books of the chancel guild.

I protested that that wasn't right. No one should have that much control over the finances of the church. She did not hold an elected position, nor did she even have a term of office, so where was the accountability? She could be funding her and Doug's winter vacations to Mexico, for all we knew — everyone looked at me — though of course that wasn't the case, just an extreme example. It happens.

But it was a lost cause. I stood alone. So every year I endured the procession of the Book, lifted high to honour the saints upon whose shoulders the church had been built. The attendance was always good, the church filled with relatives who turned out to bask in a little reflected glory and praise. Deedee knew what she was doing, all right. Who wouldn't want to have their names in that book? And every year the sanctuary was beautified with some new adornment — a reredos curtain in plush red velvet, an oak tabernacle for the reserve sacrament, an accompanying presence lamp in polished brass, a new piano.

How could anyone complain when Deedee spoke of her "secret source" for the large flower arrangements that appeared each week on the altar (though the limp funereal gladioluses were, for me, a dead giveaway), even though people were expected to make hefty donations for memorial flowers? Or who could be so brazen as to ask her what the guild actually did with the exorbitant fees it charged young couples getting married at St. Jude's?

I did not have the opportunity to warn Father David about her before he started his ministry there, following me. It has now been several years since I heard her name, so I had come to assume that, like me, he had simply caved in, taking his place somewhere down in the hold, near the engine room.

But not so. Father David, I am learning, is a fighter. He is not a scrapper, he does not go looking for a fight. But offend his principles and Father David will call down heaven and earth to join his cause. Which is what he needed against the likes of Deedee Somerset.

He, too, began raising questions about the Book and about its place of prominence in the parish anniversary service. He endured it in the early years only because he had enough battles brewing already. Also, his second year there, Deedee had found memorial money for a whole new set of vestments for him. But it still bothered him. So when some of the lesser brush fires had been brought under control, he turned to the question of the Book.

At first his concerns met with the same acquiescent solidarity I myself had encountered among the wardens and the other parish leaders. Oh, don't worry about Deedee, he was told. Sure, she could be a little pushy at times, but look at all she'd done for the church. She was a great worker and had the most wonderful ideas. But Father David was undeterred. He raised his questions publicly, both in and out of Deedee's presence. No one could say he was going behind her back. He consulted with the bishop to clarify his role as liturgical officer of the parish and reported the same to the advisory board.

Then he called Deedee and asked to come by and see her. This was not a good day, she told him, nor a good week. She would have to get back to him. He waited a week and called her again. She has hesitant. Then when she spoke her voice sounded different, sort of cold. Next Tuesday at her home, two p.m. She hung up.

She met him at the door and led him to the kitchen, which was in the back. The house was filled with the wonderful aroma of fresh baking. He settled into a kitchen chair as she poured him a coffee. He allowed himself to gaze out over the rolling hills of their large property. Doug had built several bird houses and placed them on posts at the corners of the deck. Small birds chirped merrily, scattering the seed on the deck as squirrels scurried beneath them, gathering up the overflow. It was a restful pastoral scene and Father David felt himself at ease for the difficult task at hand.

Deedee was talking about some of the "dear old ladies" of the parish, who had done so much work for the church in their day. What models they were for others, like herself. Would he like some cake? So how was he enjoying the parish? Was everything going well? How about some cream — real Devonshire cream — for his cake? She scooped some onto his plate with a spoon. Go ahead, she said, though she herself was watching her weight.

The cake parted easily with the touch of his fork. Aromatic steam rose from his coffee. She stood opposite him on the other side of the table, her hands holding the back of a kitchen chair, watching him as he took his first forkful. It was heavenly, the cream dissolving into the chocolate, releasing a rich sweetness into his mouth. He looked up. She was staring at him. He tried to swallow. His throat seemed to be constricting.

"Who do you think you are?" she began. He froze. "You waltz in here — how old are you? Thirty-five, thirty-six? I'm old enough to be your mother! What do you know about running a parish? What do you know about anything? You think because they let you wear that collar around your neck that you're something special? Well, let me tell you, mister — you're not!"

He tried again to swallow. Nothing would go down. The thought of poison crossed his mind.

"I'm going to tell you something," she went on. "These people love me. I do things for them you could never do. Oh, yes, you parade around in your fancy vestments — vestments I bought for you, by the way — thinking you're smart, preaching your smarmy sermons. But it's me they depend on, not you. You'll be gone some day, buster, just like the rest, and I'll still be here. What's the matter? Is this too hard to swallow?"

His eyes were watering. Through his blurred vision it appeared that she was going through some sort of transformation. Gone was the teenaged sweetness. Gone were the large saucer eyes. In their place was — what? — madness? Her face was contorting, her features folding into a hideous rage. He still could not swallow. Nor could he catch his breath.

He rose from the table, clutching at his throat. She seemed to be cackling. He turned and bolted for the door.

The fresh spring air slapped him in the face, releasing him from her spell. He lost his mouthful of cake over a neat row of impatiens bordering the walk to the driveway. He leaned into the car door only long enough to catch his breath, then opened it and threw himself in, backed up the drive and was gone. He did not look back.

When Father David got home, his wife, Beverley, dropped what she was doing. "David," she said, "what's wrong? You look awful." He went straight to his study, sat down and wrote a hasty letter to Deedee, dismissing her from any and all church responsibilities, copying it not only to the churchwardens but also to his archdeacon and to the bishop.

He went over to the church, locked the doors behind him, and sat by himself in the front row for a very long time. There would be fallout, he knew that. But for now he remained still, gazing upon our Lord who, in stained glass, was taking children up into his arms. His breathing slowed until, at last, he found again his inner calm.

Father David is, in many ways, a rather dull man, dutiful and humourless. But I could see him becoming a bishop some day. I could see synod surveying its options — the politically motivated, the ideologically driven, the puffed up, and the slicked down — and suddenly see here a rare man of integrity, an honest man, a man of God.

Hm. Father David as bishop? As far as I'm concerned, they should make him king.

The Great Cedar Lake Land Claim Race

In the one hundred and sixteenth year of the Diocese, Bishop Pitfield began to reign. He was sixty years old when he began to reign; and he reigned six months in the diocesan office. He died and was buried with his ancestors. The rest of the acts of Bishop Pitfield that he did, are they not written in the Book of the Annals of the Diocesan Synods? And the clergy sinned and did what was evil in the sight of the Lord.

The need for a room of one's own, for a patch of earth beneath one's feet, runs deep among the clergy. Maybe this has to do with rectories, with having to live in a house that is not your own.

Rectories have always been a mixed blessing for clergy, and to many a downright curse. You get to live in a house much larger than anything you yourself could afford, and you don't have to spend a cent on it — hydro, phone, water — nothing. In some parishes you even get your grass cut free. But neither do you get a say in how much the church does or does not spend on the upkeep of the house you and your family call home.

The turning-point for me came a few years ago when our upstairs bathroom became a topic for debate at the parish council meeting. I had raised the issue with the wardens. It related to the water damage done to that bathroom several years earlier, before our time, when there had been an electrical fire in the kitchen below. Apparently, some helpful handyman a generation or so back had cut a few corners when wiring the addition. He must have saved the parish a bundle, though the price was paid several times over after the fire, when the entire house had to be brought up to code, a costly and humiliating experience.

As part of the clean-up operation, the upstairs bathroom got a new bathtub and shower stall, with new tiles and sliding glass doors. It was lovely, but an odd bit of extravagant modernity in an otherwise dull and outdated facility, with its chipped and rust-stained sink and a toilet that refused to stop leaking from somewhere down around the base. We imagined it was only a matter of time until someone would sit down, get nice and comfortable, then suddenly plummet through the softened floorboards, waking up with a start atop the kitchen stove one floor below. It was not a pleasant prospect.

So I had humbly suggested that it was time for the parish to finish the job and complete the renovation of the upstairs bathroom. The wardens weren't sure. The church was pretty tight for money, and there was no specific provision in the budget. They'd better take it to parish council.

Well, it seemed there were a lot of folks on parish council who would have liked *their* bathrooms renovated, too, but who had to put it off, the times being what they were. Why should the rectory bathroom receive special treatment? The fact is, you can't always get what you want. Sometimes you just have to tighten your belt. Besides, would we really want to upgrade the bathroom in the rectory if it were to mean pulling back on our givings to mission work?

So the toilet leaks to this day, sinking slowly into the softened floorboards above the kitchen. The rust stains in the sink deepen with each passing season. And we will never consent to living in a rectory again.

We are not alone. I have been told that over half the clergy in the diocese now own their own homes. This is a good thing, and entirely overdue. I know it makes us less pliable and harder to place. But that happened the day the church allowed clergy to marry. Somehow we've had a mind of our own ever since.

So the need to own something, to claim a piece of the earth on which you stand, is strong among the clergy. And nowhere does it rage more fiercely than at the annual clergy conference, where we have to share rooms, the last arrival getting a wobbly cot behind a door. You learn to stake your claim early, get a bed by a window in a room down the hall from the washrooms and not right over the dining-room. It only takes your first year to figure this out. Thereafter you arrange your ride with the fastest driver, or you bring a bottle of good single malt Scotch whiskey, the better to barter with.

But the quest for a room of one's own at the clergy conference pales beside the race for a spot on the ferry going home.

You've read about the Oklahoma land claim races of the last century? The Cedar Island Church Camp sees its own version every spring. And it is not pretty.

Cedar Island is a picturesque outcrop of Canadian Shield hidden high in the province's lake district. Once the summer retreat for wealthy Americans, the island slowly gave way to hippies and homesteaders whose meagre farms seemed to specialize in esoterica such as ostriches and Peruvian pottery and curiously large crops of hemp.

There is a yoga centre on the island now, and a sailing school, a pub, and a town hall. There is also the church camp, a gift from one of the fleeing American families who didn't know what else to do with a sprawling property increasingly surrounded by squatters' camps and roving bands of bald people in saffron robes chanting songs in a foreign language while beating on drums.

The camp is an enchanting place. Sitting on the porch of the lodge on a cool summer's evening, gazing out across the lawns that roll down to the water, the waves gently lapping at the rocky shore, a soft breeze stirring the bows of the plentiful cedars (from which both the island and the lake got their names), the sweet smell of grass wafting through the trees from one of the neighbouring farms, one can achieve a sense of well-being unparalleled by, say, evening prayer.

But the real charm of Cedar Island, and of Cedar Lake itself, is the old ferry that has plied those choppy waters since 1922. The Cedar Princess shaves about an hour off the long way around that locals are forced to drive during the winter months, and delivers summer cottagers and their supplies to islands and points that are otherwise inaccessible. It is a seasonal operation that cannot possibly make any money for its owners. But it is not her usefulness that keeps the Princess in service. It is nostalgia.

The beloved old boat was long ago converted from steam to diesel fuel, and there cannot be an original plank on her long battered hull. But every year her loyal patrons arrive from all parts of the country to make that forty-minute crossing, standing outside their sedans and motor homes, leaning over the rail, chatting easily with one another like cronies, the wind in their hair, gasoline fumes in their eyes, the old ferry creaking and groaning under its happy load.

So there is no mystery to the clergy scrambling each year for a spot on the Princess. Like everyone else, they want to own a small, if fleeting, piece of her. They want to feel the rumble of that much history beneath their feet. They want to stand at the bow and command the future, if even for the few minutes it takes to arrive ashore. They want the sense of place the Princess offers.

That, and after three days with one's brother and sister clergy, debating the merits of inclusive language or the challenge of post-Christendom evangelism, or being browbeaten into the latest program for increasing membership and saving the church from its slow demise, the Cedar Princess comes to represent one's link back to the real and tangible world, a link made even more covetable by the fact that she holds only twenty-two vehicles and visits the island only three times a day. Miss the noon crossing and you stick around for supper with the maintenance staff.

There are usually twelve or fifteen carloads of clergy at the conference. Anticipating that there will be another dozen or so vehicles already on the ferry, the anxiety grows palpable during the morning hours on the last day of the conference. Before breakfast some clergy sneak out and re-position their cars in the small parking lot, so that they will be first out. During the mid-morning break others catch on and go repark *their* cars at the head of the line. By the time of the closing eucharist there are no cars in the lot at all, but instead a long line leading up the driveway to the road, some cars actually parked *on* the road, and all pointed toward the ferry dock.

Bishop Pitfield, that gentle soul, was not given to fierce looks or stern warnings. Still, the year he presided over the conference, he had made it clear that, barring some emergency, he expected the clergy to stay through to the end, which meant to the benediction at the closing eucharist. The kitchen staff had prepared box lunches for everyone, so that we could eat on the road. So, following the mid-morning break, there was only the eucharist, held informally in the fireside room, and then, straightaway, the annual race for a spot on the Cedar Princess.

The truth is, clergy are no less competitive than anyone else. They are just more subtle about it. The Passing of the Peace, for instance, looked for all the world like folks who cared for one another — warm embraces, firm handshakes, people holding each other's gaze. But to the more practised observer, you could see each point of contact was also a means of gaining a position closer to the exit.

You couldn't help but notice that as people gripped your hand and said those unctuous words — "The peace of Christ, John ... peace, Dorothy ..." — they were also using you as a pivot, twirling themselves slowly through the crowd, person by person, like so many interconnecting cogs, toward their destination. By the time the singing of the offertory hymn came, the congregation was considerably rearranged in an ungainly clump by the far door.

But they hadn't counted on Bishop Pitfield changing the routine. Ordinarily communion at the conference was distributed loosely among the clergy, one to another. But that year the bishop had chosen to administer communion from one single station in front of the altar, demanding that everyone give up their advantaged position and come forward in a single line to receive the sacrament from the bishop himself and from the two deacons who flanked him.

This had the effect of confounding their strategy. For, truly, those who had been first — that is, closest to the door — were now unequivocally last. But there was still the final blessing to get through before they got their motors running.

It wasn't clear whether Bishop Pitfield was aware of the tension in the room when he stopped before the blessing to add a few words of commendation to the camp staff, to the organizers of that year's conference and to those who would be assembling in the weeks to come to begin planning next year's conference, as well as his personal thanks for our support for him through these first months of his episcopacy. The congregation, standing now in a large circle, heads bowed, began to lose it. Murmuring could be heard. "Come on, come on," someone whispered.

Bishop Pitfield was particularly grateful to the territorial arch-deacons who were helping him become acquainted with the issues and concerns of each region of the diocese. "Oh, please," some-one moaned under his breath. And the diocesan staff members themselves — the executive archdeacon, the program staff, the secretaries — though, really, what they did was so much more than merely "secretarial."

And how fortunate he felt, indeed, for the high level of com-mitment among the clergy of the diocese. These were not easy times, he knew — "You don't know the half of it!" someone be-side me groaned — but as long as we remained one, as long as we put aside our differences and supported one another in the great privilege of serving our Lord — "All right, all right!" — then we could look ahead to a great future, to wonderful bless-ings, in the time to come.

"And so now into God's gracious keeping I commit you" — "Finally!" someone said — "be strong and of good courage, never putting off to the morrow what good works can be done today. And the blessing of God Almighty, the Father, the Son, and the Holy Spirit, be with you and with those you love, now and for ever more. Amen."

There followed the kind of explosion one might have associated with Pentecost, disciples bursting out into the streets to preach the Good News to the ends of the earth. There could be heard the starting of engines like the rush of a mighty wind, the slamming of car doors, the skidding of rubber on gravel. In a great cloud of dust, the clergy roared away as one, anxious for God's future to unfold.

All, that is, but those who were slow off the mark, those whose engines coughed or sputtered, those who forgot something back in their rooms, or who stopped to say an ill-timed farewell along the way. All these were bypassed as we tore up the dirt driveway.

Once we hit the road, it was considered bad form actually to pass another driver; so the order in which we pulled away from the camp was more or less the order in which we arrived at the dock. When we did arrive, a few minutes later, we were astounded to see Graham Yeates's car already there, at the head of the line. He had driven it there during the morning-break and then walked all the way back to the camp in time for the eucharist. You had to hand it to him, it was a bold and brilliant move.

The race was all but over. We could only await our fate when the Princess arrived. Would there be room for everyone? Who would be left behind? We circulated among our cars, chatting easily now, our destinies already sealed.

As the Princess came within view and pulled up to the dock, we were relieved to watch as a long flatbed truck disembarked, hauling a small cabin onto the island. This was a good sign, for the truck had to have been worth five or six cars anyway. Again we started our engines, inching forward as we were directed, bumper to bumper, onto the ferry. The last car was finally squeezed on and the loading ramp was raised. There was a jubilant mood onboard, as befits the self-congratulations of a winners' circle. This year, it appeared, we all might have made it.

Casually, we wound our way between the vehicles back to the stern of the boat. There at the dock, as she pulled away, was a single car, a small white compact. The driver's door opened and the driver got out to watch us go. It was Bishop Pitfield.

I couldn't make out the expression on his face. Was he angry? Was he hurt? Did he even realize there had been a race, and that he had lost? But as he grew smaller and smaller, it didn't much matter. He raised his hand to us, and waved.

One Degree of Separation

There is a popular theory called Six Degrees of Separation. It goes something like this: every man, woman, and child on the face of the earth is separated from every other man, woman, and child by no more than six people. This means that I know someone, who knows someone, who knows someone, who knows someone, who knows someone who is a tribal hunter squatted over his fire in Papua New Guinea, or a nightclub singer in Bangkok, or a shop owner in Paris, France.

I'm not sure I understand this theory. It sounds astonishing. But it is based on a simple mathematical application to the known population of the earth; that is, if there are about six billion people in the world, just keep taking the square root until you get as close as you can to the number one, which is you. The operation requires six square roots, by which we can deduce that, through just six other people, you and I know everyone in the world. Well, maybe not by name.

But when you're talking about the separation of actual people — as opposed to cold abstracted numbers of people — there is no mathematical calculation for the toll on the human heart. I know this, because this Sunday I will be announcing my resignation from the parish. I will be leaving the people who have goaded me and provoked me, inspired me and amazed me, the people who have journeyed with me, and I with them, for these eight years. Already my heart grows heavy.

Over the years I have often thought of leaving. You get stuck in a place after a while. You grow used to its compulsions, its blind spots, its beguiling sirens. Then, when you finally wake from your slumber and realize that these things don't bother you anymore, it feels like it must be time to get out, to move on. The problem is, the moment you actually make that decision, everything changes. Suddenly, you want back in again.

By this Sunday I will want to stop the fall of dominoes I have set in motion. But it will be too late. So I will be forced to enter the liturgy a liar, knowing something the congregation does not know. While I will appear the same to them, with the same idiosyncrasies they know far better than I know myself, they themselves will already have been transformed in my eyes. They will be on their way to becoming memories, familiar strangers I once knew.

Fortunately, memories are often kinder than the real thing. Which may be the reason St. Paul addressed his letters to the "saints" living in Philippi or in Colossae. Compared to the motley crew now gathered before him in his new church in some grotty Gentile outport, those folks back home were starting to look pretty good. This is because, the moment we choose to say good-bye to someone, they cease being the flesh-and-blood people who, even now, sit before us, their upturned faces waiting for the unsuspected announcement we are about to make. Already, they are icons.

Take Barry, for instance, our organist. Or the whole choir for that matter. They try so hard. And yet they remain so awful, perhaps even worse than when I first came. What kind of cruel God would place these particular well-meaning musicians in a parish that prides itself on traditional Anglican liturgy? You would think after all these years something would have given way. Either we would have fired the lot of them and started over, or they themselves would have left out of sheer embarrassment.

But the thing is, they have absolutely no idea how terrible they are. This is because they are so well loved by the congregation, and they care so much for one another, no one ever speaks the truth. Instead they compliment the "stirring" anthem, the "challenging" solo, the "tricky" passage. Implicit criticism hangs in the air, but no one reaches for it; the words themselves are filled with too much love.

So for eight years I have pulled out my hair, I have made countless hints and suggestions, I have even threatened to trade them all at the Great Parishioner Exchange, the game my clergy colleagues and I sometimes play over lunch. In all this time nothing has changed.

But approaching my last Sunday with them, which will come a few weeks hence, knowing they will attempt some sort of moving farewell anthem in my honour, I already grow misty-eyed at the thought of their butchering it. In fact, right now I would gladly give up an entire cathedral Evensong sung by professional choristers for just five minutes of this, my own battered choir —

reaching for notes only to miss them, forgetting entrances altogether, screeching at the top ends of their untrained voices.

I think we, all of us, meet most profoundly not around the areas in which we excel, but through those cracks in the surface where we are seen to fail, where we fall short. Our achievements, as real and necessary as they are, only serve to separate us further from one another, making us competitive and resentful of one another's success. It is through the cracks, the imperfections, that we see how much we need one another.

The people I will carry in my heart away from this place, the people from whom I will be most painfully separated, are not those I have liked the best — some of whom, in any case, will remain my friends — or who have made the most significant contributions to the parish. No, the ones I will miss the most will be those with whom I have shared most deeply life's hurts and failings.

And that means Lucille. Which is amazing, if I think about it, because no one has caused me more grief. No one has upset my equilibrium more, or required more damage control, or more easily deflated in a single word, a single gesture, something I may have been working on for months. But that is our bond.

How could I forget the time she stood up at vestry and shot down my plans for a fundraising campaign to pay for an assistant curate? Her boldness caught me off guard. But then, I was not aware that this was only the final manoeuvre in a campaign she had been waging since I first broached the idea with parish council some three months back.

To how many of the older members of the congregation had she complained over coffee, or at the bake table at the fall bazaar, smiling benignly to me as I walked past? We didn't need an assistant curate, she said to people, not if the rector was doing his job. It would only distract him from the things he wasn't doing already, things like visiting the elderly, and bringing back Morning Prayer. By the time of our annual vestry meeting that year, her ducks were already in a row.

But I also know that Lucille was disappointed in marriage — not once, but twice. Both husbands were drinkers, both died of cancer, both left her with less than what she had before. She had done the right thing by them both, stuck with them, nursed them through illness and through death, even through their abusive resistance to her help. Now she sits alone most days, visibly shrinking away, in a tiny apartment that looks out across a parking lot to a tall building that blocks the sun from ever reaching her shrivelling African violets.

Lucille by now has dug a hole for herself so deep that she will not climb out of it in this lifetime. There was a time when I might have "dealt with her," confronted her with her disruptive behaviour, called her on her disrespect for the rightful authority of her parish priest. But I found the only way I could truly reach her was to climb down there into the darkness from time to time and sit with her.

Now I'm glad I did. Our enmity has made us co-conspirators, gazing together into that darkness and finding not death but a friend. Yes, Lucille is now among my friends, odd as it is to hear myself say it.

There is someone else I will take with me from this place, someone the rest would hardly even recognize as being "one of them." Yet Bruce gave me the precious gift of a simple observation a few years ago when, at the prompting of his wife, he allowed himself to be prepared for confirmation.

Bruce is not an Anglican. He was raised in the Church of Scotland, the Presbyterian Church, back in industrialized Glasgow. His was a strict Calvinist upbringing, and he was all too glad to leave it when he met and married Gwen. She herself was raised in the Church of England. When they moved to Canada in the early years of their marriage she drew closer to the church, while he stayed away.

Working together in their meat shop day after day, Sunday mornings became the only time the two were apart. An active member of the altar guild, Gwen would arrive early to set up for the first service, and then stay on to help with the preparations for the main service as well. Sometimes, if we were doing something that caught her interest, she would sit in on that service, too. Meanwhile Bruce stayed at home with a second cup of coffee, reading his paper and pottering about until it was time to start lunch, which he would prepare for them every week.

Approaching their twenty-fifth wedding anniversary, Gwen had suggested a renewal of their wedding vows, something she had witnessed in her duties on the altar guild. In our preliminary discussions, it became clear Bruce was less enamoured of the idea, though not because of any squeamishness about the vows themselves. He simply thought it was not necessary to involve the church.

As we talked, I enjoyed how openly he expressed his strong opinions and vexatious questions about the church. Beneath his scepticism, I could detect a deep if somewhat unfocused faith. I wondered aloud if he might want to consider confirmation, as a way of both exploring further his issues with the church and of reaffirming his faith. We decided he and I should talk more about this.

So for about six weeks every Wednesday we would meet at the shop at noon and go across the street to the pub for a beer and a bite. There he would rail against the church for its moral hypocrisy, for its enjoyment of earthly power and riches, for its fuzzy thinking and its dim-witted clergy — present company excluded, of course. I couldn't disagree with most of what we said, so he would go on.

"You know that thing you Anglican clergy do with the cup?" he asked me one day.

"No, what thing?"

"Where you wave something over it, a hanky or something."

I gathered he was talking about the preparations, when the burse and veil are removed, folded neatly and placed off to one side. "Yes, I think so," I said.

"Well, at that moment, I always expect you to go, 'Shazam!' and pull a rabbit out of the cup."

I couldn't help but laugh. Strangely, as he said it, I knew exactly what he meant.

Bruce never was confirmed, though he and Gwen renewed their vows before a small gathering of family and friends in the church one Saturday afternoon. But every so often he has shown up with Gwen for the early service, sitting in the back row. When we get to that part in the service where I remove the burse and veil, I have to concentrate especially hard on what I am doing, knowing he is watching me, knowing that if I look up and catch his eye I will likely break out in an ungodly snort.

The theory of Six Degrees of Separation is supposed to help us recognize we are much more closely connected to each other than we thought. It is a noble sentiment. But *one* degree of separation is just about all I can handle, being the degree by which we are separated from the people we already know, and love.

Jesus prayed that we be one, even as he and the Father are one. As I get ready to announce my impending departure from this place, I cannot suppress the thought that maybe it has already happened. Maybe, deep down, we are already one, which is why separation is so hard for us to bear. Maybe all it takes for us to see it is a crack, some light, and the eyes of faith.